LITTLE READERS

FOR GUIDED READING

Collection 2
Teacher's Manual

Irene C. Fountas
Consulting Author

HOUGHTON MIFFLIN

Boston • Atlanta • Dallas • Geneva, Illinois • Palo Alto • Princeton, New Jersey

W9-BZV-754

Copyright © 1999 by Houghton Mifflin Company. All rights reserved.

Permission is hereby granted to teachers to reprint or photocopy in classroom quantities the pages or sheets in this work that carry a Houghton Mifflin Company copyright notice. These pages are designed to be reproduced by teachers for use in their classes with accompanying Houghton Mifflin materials, provided each copy made shows the copyright notice. Such copies may not be sold and further distribution is expressly prohibited. Except as authorized above, prior written permission must be obtained from Houghton Mifflin Company to reproduce or transmit this work or portions thereof in any other form or by any other electronic or mechanical means, including any information storage or retrieval system, unless expressly permitted by federal copyright law. Address inquiries to School Permissions, Houghton Mifflin Company, 222 Berkeley Street, Boston, MA 02116.

Printed in the U.S.A.

0-395-90649-0

 # Contents

Extending Readers

Blackline Masters for Record Keeping

Professional Resources

Introducing Houghton Mifflin Guided Reading

Guided reading is small-group instruction that provides opportunities for children to learn how to problem-solve as readers as they engage in reading a quality book. Considering each child's strengths and needs as a reader, you form small, temporary clusters of children and select a book that they will be able to read well. The book should provide a small amount of new challenge. After you introduce the story to children, they read the whole book or a section of a longer one. Interacting with individual children briefly as they need assistance, you support readers by reinforcing effective reading behaviors and helping them think about new ways of problem-solving as they read for understanding. Following the reading, you discuss the story and teach strategies that will be helpful to the children as readers. These teaching points are selected on the basis of your observations of how children process the text.

Strategies children develop and practice during guided reading

During guided reading, children develop strategies they will use whenever they are reading independently. They

- bring all sources of information into play to construct meaning; for example, confirming the meaning of a word by matching it to the illustration or asking if it makes sense within the context of the sentence

- use letters and sounds to identify familiar parts of unknown words

- monitor their own reading

- self-correct and problem-solve as necessary—stopping to check when something is unclear

As children read more extensively, they learn to use these strategies "in the head" to problem-solve. Your role is to observe children's use of these strategies and to coach them in overcoming any problems they encounter. With this kind of reinforcement, children's reading will become a smooth, self-extending process of comprehending and interacting with the text. This independence is the goal of guided reading.

All children have a right to literacy. With guided reading, teachers ensure that each and every child learns how to be a reader.

— Irene C. Fountas, co-author of *Guided Reading: Good First Teaching for All Children*

Program Components

Houghton Mifflin *Little Readers* — Collection 2

40 Little Readers (Collection 2) ▶

- Early Emergent
- Emergent
- Early
- Fluent
- Extending

Teacher's Manual, which includes ▶

- a lesson plan for each Little Reader
- an oral reading check for each Little Reader
- blackline masters for keeping observation records

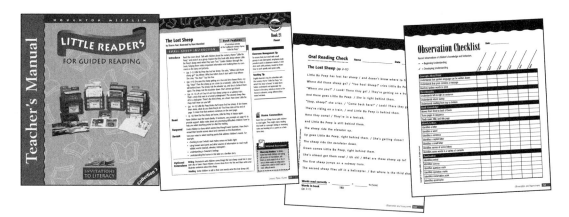

Staff Development Video that models guided reading ▶

Using the Lesson Plans

Each lesson offers a four-step teaching plan and some helpful features as described below.

Book Features Lists special aspects of each book

LESSON PLAN

1. **Introduce** Introduces the plot and any special language; focuses on particular aspects important to children's successful processing of the text: one or two words, unusual layout, text structure ("how the book works").

2. **Read** Teacher observes, prompts, and supports readers as necessary.

3. **Respond** Children's responses direct discussion.

4. **Revisit** Opportunities to discuss children's problem-solving strategies. Use your observations to determine which points to emphasize.

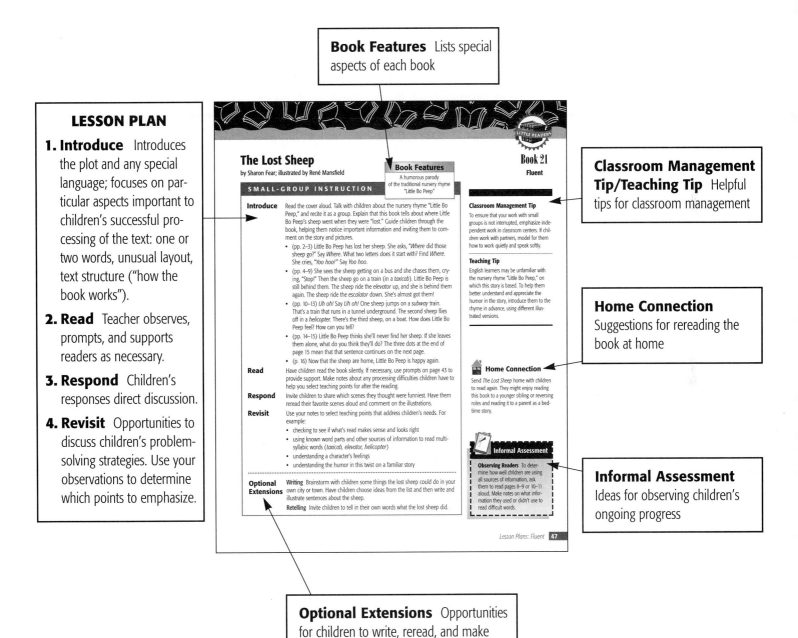

The Lost Sheep
by Sharon Fear; illustrated by René Mansfield

SMALL-GROUP INSTRUCTION

Book Features
A humorous parody of the traditional nursery rhyme "Little Bo Peep"

Book 21
Fluent

Introduce Read the cover aloud. Talk with children about the nursery rhyme "Little Bo Peep," and recite it as a group. Explain that this book tells about where Little Bo Peep's sheep went when they were "lost." Guide children through the book, helping them notice important information and inviting them to comment on the story and pictures.
- (pp. 2–3) Little Bo Peep has lost her sheep. She asks, "*Where* did those sheep go?" Say *Where*. What two letters does it start with? Find *Where*. She cries, "*Yoo hoo!*" Say *Yoo hoo*.
- (pp. 4–9) She sees the sheep getting on a bus and she chases them, crying, "Stop!" Then the sheep go on a train (in a *taxicab*). Little Bo Peep is still behind them. The sheep ride the *elevator* up, and she is behind them again. The sheep ride the *escalator* down. She's almost got them!
- (pp. 10–13) *Uh oh!* Say *Uh oh!* One sheep jumps on a *subway* train. That's a train that runs in a tunnel underground. The second sheep flies off in a *helicopter*. There's the third sheep, on a boat. How does Little Bo Peep feel? How can you tell?
- (pp. 14–15) Little Bo Peep thinks she'll never find her sheep. If she leaves them alone, what do you think they'll do? The three dots at the end of page 15 mean that that sentence continues on the next page.
- (p. 16) Now that the sheep are home, Little Bo Peep is happy again.

Read Have children read the book silently. If necessary, use prompts on page 43 to provide support. Make notes about any processing difficulties children have to help you select teaching points for after the reading.

Respond Invite children to share which scenes they thought were funniest. Have them reread their favorite scenes aloud and comment on the illustrations.

Revisit Use your notes to select teaching points that address children's needs. For example:
- checking to see if what's read makes sense and looks right
- using known word parts and other sources of information to read multi-syllabic words (*taxicab, elevator, helicopter*)
- understanding a character's feelings
- understanding the humor in this twist on a familiar story

Optional Extensions **Writing** Brainstorm with children some things the lost sheep could do in your own city or town. Have children choose ideas from the list and then write and illustrate sentences about the sheep.

Retelling Invite children to tell in their own words what the lost sheep did.

Classroom Management Tip
To ensure that your work with small groups is not interrupted, emphasize independent work in classroom centers. If children work with partners, model for them how to work quietly and speak softly.

Teaching Tip
English learners may be unfamiliar with the nursery rhyme "Little Bo Peep," on which this story is based. To help them better understand and appreciate the humor in the story, introduce them to the rhyme in advance, using different illustrated versions.

Home Connection
Send *The Lost Sheep* home with children to read again. They might enjoy reading this book to a younger sibling or reversing roles and reading it to a parent as a bedtime story.

Informal Assessment
Observing Readers To determine how well children are using all sources of information, ask them to read pages 8–9 or 10–11 aloud. Make notes on what information they used or didn't use to read difficult words.

Lesson Plans: Fluent **47**

Classroom Management Tip/Teaching Tip Helpful tips for classroom management

Home Connection Suggestions for rereading the book at home

Informal Assessment Ideas for observing children's ongoing progress

Optional Extensions Opportunities for children to write, reread, and make connections to other stories or experiences

LITTLE READERS

Choosing Texts for Readers

Successful guided reading depends upon an appropriate match between the child and the text. ▶

Houghton Mifflin Little Readers

The *Little Readers* in Collection 2 include a broad range of books, from simple stories about subjects close to children's experiences to chapter books and informational texts. Stories at the beginning of the Collection are short and simple with clear illustrations and strong natural language patterns to support beginning readers. As children grow in their ability to process text, the complexity and variety of the stories increase as well. The books provide a balance between challenge and ease, allowing children to make successful progress without frustration. They are leveled to indicate their gradual increase in challenge. This ensures that you will find the appropriate level of text for each child in your guided reading groups. When in doubt about a starting place, choose the easier of the texts in question.

Early Emergent		Emergent		Early		Fluent		Extending	
1. Things I Can Do	B	5. Mrs. Sato's Hens	D	10. The Three Billy Goats Gruff	G	16. Nobody Listens to Andrew	I	30. Frog and Toad All Year	K
2. The Fox on the Box	C	6. The Good Bad Cat	D	11. Washing the Dog	G	17. Bookstore Cat	I	31. Frog and Toad Together	K
3. At the Supermarket	C	7. A Mosquito Buzzed	E	12. The Crazy Quilt	G	18. Digby	I	32. Too Many Babas	K
4. I Want a Pet	C	8. The Secret Friend	E	13. How to Make a Mud Pie	H	19. Mrs. Murphy's Bears	I	33. Zack's Alligator	K
		9. Smile, Baby!	F	14. Lift the Sky Up	H	20. Who Lives Here?	I	34. Here Comes the Strikeout	K
				15. The Mystery of the Missing Red Mitten	H	21. The Lost Sheep	I	35. Jamaica and Brianna	K
						22. Anansi's Narrow Waist	I	36. Thank You, Amelia Bedelia	L
						23. Bears, Bears, Bears	I	37. Amelia Bedelia and the Surprise Shower	L
						24. Happy Birthday, Danny and the Dinosaur!	J	38. Bobo's Magic Wishes	L
						25. Henry and Mudge: The First Book	J	39. What's It Like to Be a Fish?	M
						26. Henry and Mudge Get the Cold Shivers	J	40. A Picture Book of Helen Keller	M
						27. Dogs at Work	J		
						28. Addie's Bad Day	J		
						29. The Grandma Mix-up	J		

Collection 2 is organized into five broad groups or categories: Early Emergent, Emergent, Early, Fluent, and Extending. The chart on page 8 lists the titles within each group. Each group or stage contains a gradient of difficulty, from easier to harder. Letters indicate approximate guided reading levels as provided in *Guided Reading: Good First Teaching for All Children,* by Irene C. Fountas and Gay Su Pinnell, published by Heinemann, © 1996. You are encouraged to refer to this book for a comprehensive discussion of guided reading and for an expanded booklist that will help you match the strengths of your children with many familiar books for beginning readers.

Selecting an appropriate text for each child

Guided reading is a flexible instructional process, meant to support each child's changing strengths and needs over time. To support this process, it is possible to identify reading behaviors in groups of children and appropriately match those characteristics with books that will meet the needs of the reader. The chart below uses representative books from each category to illustrate how the books in Collection 2 have been selected and leveled to meet the needs of readers at various stages of reading development.

Early Emergent	Emergent	Early	Fluent	Extending
Example: *Things I Can Do* (Level B)	Example: *A Mosquito Buzzed* (Level E)	Example: *Lift the Sky Up* (Level H)	Example: *Henry and Mudge: The First Book* (Level J)	Example: *What's It Like to Be a Fish?* (Level M)
• simple, uncluttered text • close picture/text match • clear, recognizable photographs • one sentence on each page • natural language patterns • use of simple, high-frequency words	• clear, easy-to-follow story line • simple narrative story • inviting illustrations that clearly support the text • repeated episodes and language • includes simple dialogue • small twist at the end that keeps readers engaged	• more than one event in the story • more complex concepts • sentence structure more complex • clear problem and resolution • illustrations assist the reader in understanding story events	• familiar experiences • divided into chapters • layout of text varies across pages • more than one character in the story • clear problem and resolution • more complex sentences and wider range of vocabulary	• nonfiction about a single topic • more complex concepts • longer paragraphs and more complex sentence structure • text includes specialized vocabulary • diagrams provide visual support for information in text

Assessing Progress

Ongoing observation and systematic record keeping give you the data necessary to continually revise and inform your teaching, based on each child's growth and needs. No single assessment tool can adequately measure a child's progress. The information below offers suggestions about a variety of approaches that will support children and inform your teaching at every step.

Additional Resources

Marie Clay's book, *An Observation Survey of Early Literacy Achievement,* provides valuable, practical information on assessment procedures for guided reading. We also recommend using Houghton Mifflin's *Emergent Literacy Survey* to assess children's early reading behaviors. For more information on other assessment sources, see the list of professional resources on page 126.

Elements of children's reading behavior to observe

The important operations to observe are the following:

- letter identification
- concepts about print
- word recognition
- writing vocabulary
- ability to hear and record sounds in words
- actual reading of text

Each of these behaviors can be observed formally, using a variety of published literacy surveys, and anecdotally, using checklists, daily notes, and other informal evidence.

Recording observed information

Informal, anecdotal evidence can be recorded in many ways. This manual provides two forms, an Observation Checklist (pp. 121–122) and an Informal Observation Record (p. 125), that you can use to record informal data about children.

Observation Checklist	Informal Observation Record
There are a number of ways to use this form. You might • keep it handy during your guided reading groups to record behaviors you notice in individual children • use it after taking an oral reading check to record skills the child has mastered and others he or she needs to work on • use it as a reference for creating your own list of skills and behaviors tailored to the needs of your class Be aware that the list does not include all the reading behaviors you may notice in children. Use it as a broad guide for observing children's progress.	This form provides a place to make detailed comments and to list any specific skills you observe children using as they read and revisit the text. The notes you take will help you • choose teaching points to focus on during guided reading lessons • see ways to guide each child based on where they are right now • organize groups so that children receive the maximum support from their peers as well as from you • observe and chart each child's progress toward independence

Formal assessment of literacy

We recommend using the Houghton Mifflin *Emergent Literacy Survey* and oral reading checks to determine children's strengths and identify which of the leveled texts will best suit each child's individual needs. The *Emergent Literacy Survey* assesses children's achievement in the areas of phonemic awareness; reading concepts, including concepts of print; letter naming; word recognition; and writing. You can also use this survey to chart children's progress and learn more about their growth in these areas over time. Oral reading checks are described in further detail below.

Oral reading checks

An oral reading check is a written coding of a child's reading of a text, taken by a teacher or other trained personnel. The method described here is similar to Marie Clay's running record. This manual provides only an introduction to the basic principles. For a complete explanation of running records, we recommend that you use Clay's book, *An Observation Survey of Early Literacy Achievement,* in addition to the information provided here.

Oral reading checks will be helpful to you in these ways:

- Scores from oral reading checks will help match each child to an appropriate level of book—one in which the child can read with an accuracy rate of 90% or above. Accuracy rate provides one indicator; the real measure is in the quality of the processing observed.

- Analysis of recorded miscues, substitutions, and self-corrections in reading provides information about individual instructional needs as well as strengths in use of strategies and sources of information in texts.

- Files of oral reading checks made throughout the year facilitate flexible grouping.

- They provide valuable information for conferring with children and parents.

- Observation of how a child reads a text—including phrasing, expression, and use of a variety of cues, checking to be sure all sources of information fit or to determine when attempts don't make sense—provides evidence of comprehension.

> **Take Oral Reading Checks to**
> - ensure an appropriate text choice
> - learn about each child's needs and strengths
> - make grouping decisions
> - provide concrete evidence of a child's reading progress
> - assess comprehension
> - identify areas that need support and additional instruction

Assessing Progress *(continued)*

Selecting text samples for oral reading checks

When first organizing guided reading groups, you will need to use text that children have not read before. Select a book or, if using a longer book, choose a passage of approximately 100 words for the child to read aloud to you. Aim for a sample that may be a bit easy, and record the child's reading and your comments.

For subsequent records, it's best to use text that the child has read the day before. This ensures that the child is reading for meaning; therefore, the record will provide a reliable sample of the child's reading behaviors. If you wish to use the Little Readers to take oral reading checks, see the blackline masters on pages 81–120.

How to take an oral reading check

Introduce the book or passage to the child by reading the title and/or making a short generalizing statement about the book. Then have the child read the book, or the chosen section, aloud independently, monitoring his or her own reading. On the sample page, enter a notation above each word as the child reads or attempts to read it. Use an established series of marks and shorthand notations to mark for the following:

- each word read correctly
- substitutions or miscues
- omissions or added words
- self-corrections
- repetitions
- attempts at reading a word
- words you tell the child

Add more detailed information about children's use of strategies, such as noticing errors and their use of meaning and structural or visual information, and any other comments you feel necessary, immediately after the reading. Make notes about the child's use of phrasing and expression.

How often to take oral reading checks

During the first few weeks of school, set aside time to take one or more oral reading checks for each child. These records will provide a basis for organizing the first guided reading groups. Once you have begun guided reading, schedule oral reading checks at various points in time to inform your teaching. This may mean weekly for one group or child and monthly for others. Many teachers use the time immediately before or after guided reading to take one or two oral reading checks. At the earliest stages, more frequent records may be helpful.

Scoring and analyzing oral reading checks

After marking the sample text, tally the number of words read correctly. Divide that number by the total number of words in the sample. This will give you the child's accuracy rate as a percentage. In general, if the child's accuracy rate is 90% or better, the book and others of the same level are probably appropriate for guided reading for that child. If the accuracy rate is below 90%, the child should probably be reading a book from an easier level. To inform future instruction, examine the types of errors the child made most often and their probable causes. For example, if the word *said* was read instead of *sail,* the child probably neglected to use meaning or structure in the attempt, and did not notice the error.

Accuracy rate provides a general guideline for analyzing oral reading checks. However, what is even more important is the child's use of reading strategies and his or her ability to read with phrasing and fluency. For example, a child can read a text with slow, labored processing but with a high accuracy level. This information indicates that in order to reach fluency the child needs more experience with this level of text.

Behaviors to look at to evaluate fluency

Rate of reading, reading in phrased units, accuracy, and expression are some indicators to listen for as children read. As children progress through leveled texts, their reading should be smooth and expressive and show evidence of their ability to understand and problem-solve efficiently and independently. This behavior provides one indication that a child is ready to move on to more challenging texts.

Recording information about children's fluency

Record your observations

- during oral reading checks
- during the Read portion of a guided reading lesson
- when children read aloud
- from tape-recordings of children reading familiar books

A Note About Fluency

Fluency is one measure of the development of a child's self-extending process of reading. Children need to read leveled texts fluently before moving on to higher levels of challenge. Children may also skip levels, depending on how their fluency develops as they read the texts.

Managing the Classroom During Guided Reading

Successful management of guided reading depends upon

- setting up initial groups and keeping them flexible as children develop

- careful organization of the classroom

- a schedule for incorporating the lessons into your literacy time frame

- meaningful activities for children to engage in independently while you teach a small group

Setting up the initial guided reading groups

Decide on the purpose and scope of guided reading in your classroom. Many teachers begin with one group and gradually add groups as children learn to work independently.

During the first several weeks of school, observe children as they engage in reading and writing activities. Formally assess each child's reading achievement as well, using the Houghton Mifflin *Emergent Literacy Survey* and an oral reading check. See pages 11–12.

Organize children into guided reading groups of two to six children, according to their reading strengths. As a starting point, find the level of text that each child can read with 90% accuracy or better and with good processing. For example, if you find that a few children are able to read *Mrs. Murphy's Bears* with 90% accuracy or better, you might group them together and start them off with a Fluent text that is close to *Mrs. Murphy's Bears* in the level of challenge it presents. When in doubt about a starting place, choose the easier of the texts in question and adjust accordingly.

There is no specific number of groups within a classroom. You may have as many as four or five, and that number should change depending on the progress of individual children. You will want to analyze how well each child processes text at a particular level for several days, until you determine that the child is fluent at that level of challenge. Individual children or an entire group may need a higher level text, and you may need to reorganize accordingly. Keeping your groups flexible, dynamic, and centered always on the progress of individual readers will help you give children the support they need.

NOTE

Ideally, *Little Readers* are reserved for guided reading and not read by children before the book is presented to them in a guided reading group. Therefore, you'll need a place to store the *Little Readers* until you use them with children. Once the book is read, however, add it to the crate or browsing basket for children to read during their independent reading time.

Setting up the classroom

Classroom set-up depends upon available space and individual teaching styles. Many teachers prefer to have available an area for meeting with a large group, several small-group spaces, a space reserved specifically for guided reading groups, and independent work areas or centers—a listening/reading corner, a writing center, and so on.

Providing for the guided reading space

A low-key, pleasant environment is essential. Each classroom is different, but here is a list of items that many teachers use in their guided reading areas.

- a quiet space with table and chairs
- pencils, journals, or writing materials
- chart paper and markers
- magnetic letters and tray
- blank sentence strips
- correction tape, masking tape
- scissors
- cards to add to word wall

Adding guided reading to a daily schedule

The independent routines you establish for children should make it possible for you to take small groups aside and conduct guided reading during your regular reading block. How much time you spend on guided reading will depend on your goals and the needs of your students, the number of flexible guided reading groups in your class, the amount of time in your school day devoted to reading/language arts, and the other activities within that block of time. Each guided reading block should take approximately 15–30 minutes. While one group is working with you, give other work groups a choice from the routines you have taught them.

Sample Daily Schedule

Minutes	
5–10	Morning meeting
10–15	Teacher read-aloud or shared reading of song, chant, or rhyme
35–45	Core literature (Big Books and Anthology) including whole-class activities for reading, responding, or developing skills from age-appropriate literature
30–45	Flexible groups (guided reading or skill development)
20–35	Writing instruction

Record Keeping
See the "List of Books Read for Guided Reading," pages 123–124, for keeping track of the books each child has read.

Managing the Classroom *(continued)*

Establishing independent literacy routines

Children in the class who are not in the group need to be involved in independent, meaningful literacy tasks. Prepare children for this independence by establishing certain routines early in the year. Here are some routines that many teachers find helpful.

LITERACY ROUTINES	
Partner Reading	Partners reread a familiar or favorite book they've participated in during shared reading. Teach children how to share the reading with each other, taking turns reading and turning pages.
Self-Selected Reading	Children can choose books from the browsing baskets in the reading corner. Establish an expectation that readers will work quietly and independently during this time. You might also place a book log in the corner so that children might log in the books they read.
Word or Letter Searches	Children search newspaper headlines, magazines, and catalogs for specific letters or words, either of your choice or their own. They can circle or highlight these letters as they go. Possible searches include: • short and long words • words that begin or end with a certain sound or letter • words they can read • words that appear on the word wall • naming words or action words • words with a certain pattern, for example, *-ing* or *-ed* endings • words with two, three, or four letters
Journal Writing	Children can make daily or weekly journal entries on a topic of their choosing. Later, if they wish, they may want to share their writing with others in the class.

Teaching the routines

Teach one routine at a time, following these steps:

- Model the routine. Guide children through each step. Let them practice as you watch and offer assistance.

- Review the routine. Let children follow it on their own. Observe them and provide gentle, corrective feedback as necessary.

- Have children practice the routine while you work on something else.

Children will typically master these routines in several days, though some will need longer. Once children have learned two or three routines, you can begin adding guided reading to your schedule. As children increase the time they are able to work independently, expand guided reading lessons accordingly.

Making grouping decisions

Use oral reading checks and your observations to determine when individual children are ready to read more challenging texts. Assess children's accuracy rates by taking oral reading checks (see pages 11–12). An accuracy rate consistently in the easy range of 95% or above, with phrased, smooth processing, indicates that the child is probably ready to move on to the next level of challenge. Accuracy considerably lower than 90% may mean that the child will work best with a different group of children and another level of text.

Knowing when to move a child depends on daily anecdotal information as well. Use your notes and observations to compare a particular child's reading behavior to the information given on pages 18, 24, 32, 40, and 60. This will help you determine whether a child is fluent at a particular level of text.

Using centers in the classroom

You may want to use centers in addition to independent routines. Typical centers are a listening center and a reading center or a combination of the two. As children begin reading independently, they can use these two centers as places to read familiar books from both shared and guided reading. You might include real-world items, such as menus, advertisements, children's magazine articles, picture dictionaries, or even store circulars to capture children's attention as readers.

Additional centers might provide space for

- puppets and dramatic play

- an art and writing area

The focus of guided reading is on each child's progress and not on the group as a whole. The goal is to support each child's progress using an efficient, small-group format, *not* to sort children by ability on a permanent basis.

Which Group?

Place children in groups by using your understanding of

- each child's reading strengths and needs

- the difficulty of the text

- which texts will support each child's progress from where he is to where he needs to go

Early Emergent

The information on this page is meant to help you select appropriately leveled texts for children to develop effective reading behaviors. The descriptions are broad, and you should expect some overlap between Early Emergent and other reading stages. To identify each child's approximate reading stage and to provide the child with appropriate books, use your observation notes and the oral reading checks you have recorded for that child.

Most Early Emergent readers

▸ have some understanding of basic concepts about books (front and back cover, title, title page, beginning, middle, and end) and about print directionality (front-to-back, top-to-bottom)

▸ use information from details in the pictures to confirm their predictions about story events

▸ recognize some letters and their sounds and read a few high-frequency words

▸ can, by the end of Early Emergent, match one-to-one between voice and print by pointing as they read

▸ can figure out a few unfamiliar words with support and on their own

Children who exhibit many but not necessarily all of the above behaviors should be able to successfully process and yet be appropriately challenged by books in an Early Emergent group.

Books suitable for Early Emergent readers have text that is set in large, clear type with good spacing between words and between lines. They include informational as well as fictional texts, and they have a simple story line or concept that is usually familiar to children. Pictures strongly support the text on each page, and the language structures and vocabulary reflect the children's own oral language. In some books, a sentence pattern may repeat throughout with one or two word changes on each page to advance the story. Commas and exclamation points are used to aid meaning and expression, and a vocabulary of high-frequency words is developed. Books in this stage are

Things I Can Do

The Fox on the Box

At the Supermarket

I Want a Pet

Coaching to Problem-Solve

An important aspect of a successful guided reading program is the careful language a teacher uses to coach the **Early Emergent** reader to problem-solve in the reading process. The first step is critical—choosing appropriately leveled books to help ensure that the text is supportive to the reader, offering a proper balance between challenge and ease. During and after reading, your job is to intervene as necessary from time to time to provide support for the successful reading behaviors evidenced by the reader. You may also need to remind the reader to use all available information if a problem arises. Here is a sampling of effective coaching statements that will help Early Emergent readers as they learn to process text.

► To ensure that the child is engaging with the print, and not simply relying on the predictability or repetition of the text:
Put your finger under each word as you read. Did you have enough words? Did you have too many?

► To help readers attend to high-frequency words:
Can you find the word _____? Put your finger under it.

► To encourage children to use all available sources of information:
Look at the picture. Can it help you?

► To support smoothly phrased reading:
Read that as if you were talking.

Note: *For a comprehensive discussion of coaching statements or prompts to guide the reading and for a more extensive list of leveled books for early readers, see* Guided Reading: Good First Teaching for All Children, *by Irene C. Fountas and Gay Su Pinnell, published by Heinemann.*

Book 1
Early Emergent

Things I Can Do
by Peter Sloan and Sheryl Sloan

Book Features
Familiar, everyday activities; close text/photo match

Classroom Management Tip

Early in the year, establish a few simple routines for children to follow as they move in and out of guided reading groups and other activities. This will help to minimize interruptions to guided reading as children work outside the group.

Home Connection

Children can take *Things I Can Do* home and read it to family members. Suggest that children and their families talk about things they would like to learn how to do, as well as things they know how to do already.

Informal Assessment

Observing Readers As children read, note whether they understand basic book and text parts—front cover, title, title page, and where to begin reading—and whether they can identify a word and a sentence.

SMALL-GROUP INSTRUCTION

Introduce   Read the title and point out the girl in the cover photo. Invite children to talk a little about things they can do, like the girl can. Encourage them to use the words *I can*. Explain to children that in this book the girl tells about lots of things she can do and that the photos show her doing them. Point out the word *I* on the cover, and tell children that each sentence in the book begins with this word. Some suggestions follow for helping children notice important aspects of the book, such as its language structure and use of photos. Invite conversation that will build children's interest, pointing out words shown in italic, if helpful.

- (p. 2) The girl says, "I can ride a bike." Say the word *can*. What letter do you expect to see first? Find *can*. The word *can* is on every page.
- (pp. 3–6) The girl can *catch*, dig a hole, and lots of other things.
- (p. 7) Turn to page 7. Find the word *can*. She can paint a picture.
- (p. 8) On the last page, she says, "I can do lots of things." Say *lots*. What letter do you expect to see first in *lots*? Find it. Now read about all the things the girl says she can do.

Read   As children read the story softly or silently, have them point to each word, watching to see how well they match spoken words to written text. Use appropriate prompts (see page 19) to support readers when necessary. Make notes about any processing difficulties children may have.

Respond   Invite children to talk about why the girl looks happy. What things can they do that make them happy?

Revisit   Using your observation notes, choose teaching points that will help children develop their reading strategies. Some possibilities include:

- using letter/sound knowledge to read new words
- using photos to check what's been read
- reading high-frequency words (*I, can, a, do*)
- understanding that spoken language can be written down

Things I Can Do provides good practice for children in matching their oral language to printed text. Encourage children to reread this book on their own.

Optional Extensions   **Interactive Writing** Help children write a book titled *Things We Can Do*. They can write and illustrate one or two pages each, using their own names in place of *I* in the book's sentence pattern. Compile the pages into a book, and have children write the last page together: *We can do lots of things.*

Rereading Have partners read alternating pages to each other. Then ask each of them to think of and say a new sentence that tells something they can do.

The Fox on the Box

by Barbara Gregorich; illustrated by Robert Masheris

Book 2
Early Emergent

Book Features
Predictable text
with strong picture support

SMALL-GROUP INSTRUCTION

Introduce Read the title and point out the illustration on the cover. Explain that this book is about a fox who did a lot of things with a box. In the end, the box sat on the fox. Guide children through particular aspects of the book, helping them notice important information in its words, language structure, and pictures. Some suggestions follow. Story words you may wish to point out for some readers are in italic.

- (p. 3) The fox sat on the box. Say *on*. What letter would you expect to see first? Find the word *on*.
- (pp. 4–5) Turn to page 5. In this part of the story, the fox *ate* on the box.
- (pp. 6–7) Turn to page 7. The fox *played* on the box.
- (pp. 8–9) On this page, the fox *jumped over* the box. Say *over*. What letter comes first? Find the word *over*.
- (pp. 10–16) In the last part of the story, the fox jumped on the box. The box flew in the air and then the box sat on the fox.

Read Have children read the story softly or silently, pointing crisply under each word. Use appropriate prompts (see page 19) to support readers when necessary. Make notes about any processing difficulties children have for later use in the lesson.

Respond Ask children what they think was funny about this story. Discuss with them how the fox might have felt at the end of the story.

Revisit Use your observation notes to select teaching points that will be helpful for children. For example:

- pointing to one word and saying one word each time
- recognizing and reading words that describe actions (*sat, ate, played, jumped*)
- using illustrations to confirm particular words
- reading and understanding words that indicate position (*on, over*)

Because of the natural language pattern, *The Fox on the Box* provides opportunities for children to develop fluency while reading for meaning. Encourage them to choose the book from the browsing box during independent reading.

Optional Extensions **Writing** Children can write about other things the fox might do on, or around, the box. Have them complete this sentence and illustrate it:

The fox _____ _____ the box.

Reading Have children read *The Fox on the Box* aloud to a partner.

Classroom Management Tip

Remember to keep guided reading groups flexible. Check children's progress frequently and re-form groups to accommodate children's changing levels of progress.

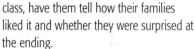

Home Connection

Invite children to take home *The Fox on the Box* to read aloud to family members. When they return the book to class, have them tell how their families liked it and whether they were surprised at the ending.

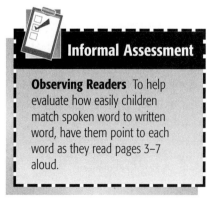

Informal Assessment

Observing Readers To help evaluate how easily children match spoken word to written word, have them point to each word as they read pages 3–7 aloud.

Book 3

Early Emergent

At the Supermarket

by Peter Sloan and Sheryl Sloan

Classroom Management Tip

Establish the guided reading routine and guide children into purposeful independent reading activities early in the year. Take a few minutes at the start of guided reading sessions to review children's understanding of the independent activities they may choose from while you're working with a small group.

Home Connection

Children can take *At the Supermarket* home to read to family members. Suggest that the next time they go to the supermarket with a family member, they compare their shopping trip with the one in the book.

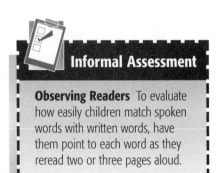

Informal Assessment

Observing Readers To evaluate how easily children match spoken words with written words, have them point to each word as they reread two or three pages aloud.

SMALL-GROUP INSTRUCTION

Introduce Read aloud the title and the authors' names. Talk with children about what a *supermarket* is and what they do when they go there. (They may know it by another name, such as *grocery store* or *food store*.) Explain that the boy in the photograph helped his mother at the supermarket by putting the food into the shopping cart. Show page 2 and read it. Tell children that each page of the book tells something different that the boy put into the shopping cart. Then, when his mother paid for the food, he pushed the cart. Guide children through the book, engaging them in conversation and helping them notice information in the words and photographs.

- (pp. 2–5) The boy says, "I put the *apples* into the shopping cart." Say *put*. What letter do you expect to see first? Point to the word. (Help children notice that each photograph shows what the boy put into the cart, so they can use the photos to confirm their reading.)

- (p. 8) On the last page, Mom *paid* for the food, and the boy *pushed* the shopping cart. Say *pushed*. What letter do you expect it to start with? Find the word and point to it.

Read Have children read the book softly, pointing with their finger. Observe children as they read, and intervene as necessary. (See page 19 for suggested prompts.) Use notes from your observations to select teaching points for Revisit.

Respond Invite children to comment on the book and on the foods the boy and his mother bought. Which of these foods would they buy at the supermarket? What else would they buy?

Revisit Based on your observations, select teaching points that address children's needs. For example:

- reading high-frequency words (*I, put, the, and*)
- using picture clues to confirm meaning
- accurately matching spoken words to printed words

Rereading encourages the confidence that leads to fluency. After a first reading, suggest that each child reread the book quietly with a classmate who has also read it before.

....

Optional Extensions **Writing** Invite children to write and illustrate their own versions of *At the Supermarket* using the sentence pattern from the book:
I put the _____ into the shopping cart.

I Want a Pet

by Barbara Gregorich; illustrated by Rex Schneider

Book Features

Simple book language and structure

SMALL-GROUP INSTRUCTION

Introduce
Read the cover. Tell children that the boy in this story wants a pet. He sees many animals to choose from. They are all different colors, but he wants a green pet. In the end we'll see if he finally gets one. Guide children through particular aspects of the book, helping them notice important information in its language, pictures, story, or words. Pointing out the words in italics may benefit some readers.

- (title page) The boy is going to look for a pet. The sign says *ENTRANCE, THE PET WORLD*. Where else have you seen *ENTRANCE* signs?
- (pp. 2–3) In the first part of the story, the boy says he wants a pet.
- (pp. 4–11) He doesn't want a *very big* (*brown, black, white*) pet. See how the *very big* (*brown, black, white*) animals are going away.
- (pp. 12–13) He wants a *green* pet. The exclamation point at the end of the sentence shows that the boy is excited.
- (pp. 14–15) He says he wants two green pets—a chameleon and a parrot.
- (p. 16) The sign says *EXIT, Come Back Soon*. Where is the boy going with his two pets?

Read
Have children read the story softly or silently, pointing to each word. Intervene when necessary, using appropriate prompts from page 19. Make notes about any processing difficulties children may have to help you select important teaching points after the reading.

Respond
Discuss with children the animals they saw in the book. Ask them which of these animals they would choose as a pet and encourage them to explain the reasons for their choices.

Revisit
Use your notes to select teaching points that will be helpful. For example:

- matching one spoken word to one written word
- using information from details in the pictures to confirm predictions about story events
- using initial consonant clusters in words to confirm (*brown, black, green*)
- recognizing what sounds right and makes sense
- recognizing that exclamation points show strong feeling

Have children reread this book with a partner.

Optional Extensions
Writing Have children write a group book about pets they want. They can complete these sentences and draw pictures to go with them: *I do not want a _____ _____ _____ pet. I want a _____ pet.*

Teaching Tip

The color words are critical to understanding the story. Write each color word (*brown, black, white, green*) on an index card. Help children read the words and then find classroom objects of that color to label with cards.

FYI

Share with children the fact that chameleons change color when the light or temperature changes or when they become scared. Point out that the humor in the story is due to the fact that *this* chameleon changes color depending on what type of pet the boy wants.

🏠 Home Connection

Encourage children to take *I Want a Pet* home. Suggest that they discuss with their families any experiences family members may have had in choosing a pet. Have them share this information when they return the books to school.

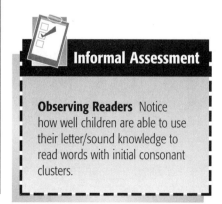

Informal Assessment

Observing Readers Notice how well children are able to use their letter/sound knowledge to read words with initial consonant clusters.

Emergent

The information on this page is meant to help you select appropriately leveled texts for children to develop effective reading behaviors. The descriptions are broad, and you should expect some overlap between Emergent and other reading stages. To identify each child's approximate reading stage and to provide the child with appropriate books, use your observation notes and the oral reading checks you have recorded for that child.

Most Emergent readers

▶ continue to use and expand problem-solving strategies developed at the Early Emergent stage

▶ depend less on finger pointing as they read

▶ are beginning to read in phrases, which will help them read more fluently

▶ make accurate predictions about story events

▶ can problem-solve more independently, using various sources of information (letters and their sounds, known words and word parts, language structure, and what makes sense)

▶ know most letter names and most of their sounds

▶ are able to recognize a few more words

▶ can compare elements such as characters, events, or endings from different books

Children who exhibit many but not necessarily all of the above behaviors should be able to successfully process and yet be appropriately challenged by books in an Emergent group.

Books suitable for Emergent readers feature clear, well-spaced type with a gradually increasing amount of text per page. They have question marks and simple dialogue set in quotation marks, and some use different kinds of print in the text or art for special purposes. In some, the sentences may be longer and more complex than in the Early Emergent books, but many continue to have repeated sentence patterns in which only one or two words change on each page. They may contain more than one character or episode. While most have concepts that are familiar to children, some topics may lead children to new, unexplored areas of interest. Books in this stage are

Mrs. Sato's Hens
The Good Bad Cat
A Mosquito Buzzed
The Secret Friend
Smile, Baby!

LITTLE READERS

Coaching to Problem-Solve

The **Emergent** reader has moved into more challenging texts. It is important to note that just as the descriptions or categories of reading stages have much overlap, the coaching statements or prompts appropriate for Early Emergent readers may still be of help to Emergent readers. The sampling of appropriate coaching statements that follows may be helpful for Emergent readers as they process text.

- To help readers use what they already know and apply it to new information:
  Do you know another word that starts like that? Does that help?

- To encourage children to construct meaning as they read:
  Try that again. Does it make sense? What would make sense?

- To ensure that readers begin to monitor their own reading behaviors:
  Go back and read that again. Does it sound right?

- To support effective reading behaviors:
  I really liked the way you figured that out.

Note: *For a comprehensive discussion of coaching statements or prompts to guide the reading and for a more extensive list of leveled books for early readers, see* Guided Reading: Good First Teaching for All Children, *by Irene C. Fountas and Gay Su Pinnell, published by Heinemann.*

Book 5

Emergent

Mrs. Sato's Hens

by Laura Min; illustrated by Benrai Huang

Book Features

A counting book in story form; progression of numbers and days of the week

SMALL-GROUP INSTRUCTION

Classroom Management Tip

To keep the guided reading groups flexible, check children's progress frequently and change the groups when necessary to accommodate individual children's changing levels of progress.

Home Connection

Have children take *Mrs. Sato's Hens* home to read aloud. Suggest that after they read, they recall with a family member something they did together on each successive day of the previous week.

Informal Assessment

Observing Readers As children reread the book, notice whether they make use of repeated language structure and patterns to help them read more smoothly, quickly, and fluently.

Introduce   Read aloud the title and the author's and illustrator's names. Explain that in this book a girl tells about what she and Mrs. Sato did together one week. They counted eggs every day except on Saturday, when they didn't count any eggs. Help children focus on aspects of the book's language, words, and other important information as you guide them through the text. Some suggestions follow.

- (p. 2) The story begins on *Sunday,* when a girl went to see Mrs. Sato's hens. Say *On.* What letter do you expect it to start with? Find it. The last name of the woman, Sato, has a little mark and a small *s* at the end. That shows that the hens belonged to Mrs. Sato. Say *Mrs. Sato's hens.*
- (p. 3) The girl says, "On Monday we *counted* two white eggs."
- (pp. 4–7) The girl tells about the eggs that she and Mrs. Sato counted on each day. They counted three brown, four speckled, five small, and six big eggs. The words *brown* and *speckled* tell what the eggs looked like. On page 5, the picture of the eggs shows that *speckled* means spotted.
- (p. 8) On Saturday, the girl says, they didn't count any eggs. Why didn't they? Yes, all the eggs hatched, so Mrs. Sato had many little chicks instead of eggs.

Read   Have children read the book softly or silently on their own. Support readers as necessary, using appropriate prompts from page 25. Make notes about any processing difficulties children may have, and use them to help you choose teaching points to focus on after they read.

Respond   Ask children to retell the story in their own words, holding up fingers to indicate the number of eggs to help them keep track of the sequence.

Revisit   Use your observation notes to select teaching points that will be the most helpful. Some possibilities are:

- checking the pictures and rereading for meaning when new words don't sound or look right
- recognizing that some of the words in a sentence pattern may change as the pattern is repeated
- reading number words (*two* through *six*) and names of the days of the week

Optional Extensions   **Interactive Writing/Rereading** Have children reread the story. Ask volunteers to write in a "calendar" format what Mrs. Sato and the girl did each day for a week as the children reread the book aloud. Children can use the "calendar" as a prompt for retelling the story to other groups or classes.

The Good Bad Cat

by Nancy Antle; illustrated by John Sandford

Book 6

Emergent

Book Features

Realistic fiction
with strong support
in richly detailed picures

SMALL-GROUP INSTRUCTION

Introduce   Read aloud the cover and title page. Explain that this book tells about a cat that is both good and bad. It is a bad cat when it runs around and upsets things. It is a good cat in the end when it gets rid of a mouse. Invite children to look at the picture on the title page. Explain that the men are quietly playing chess, a game like checkers. Have children describe the cat and what it is doing. Tell them that this scene will change when the cat chases a ball and then a mouse. As you guide children through the book, help them understand how it works by focusing on the important words and other information in its pictures and language. Some suggestions:

- (pp. 2–7) First, the cat ran under a chair, chasing a ball. Say *under*. What letter would you expect to see first? Find it. Since the cat upset the chair, the man called it a bad cat. Then the cat ran other places. Look at the pictures to see where it ran.

- (pp. 8–9) Then the cat saw a *mouse*. And so did everyone else.

- (pp. 10–11) The artist painted the cat and the mouse in three different places to show that they were moving. The mouse ran under, over, and across some of the same places that the cat ran when it chased the ball.

- (pp. 12–15) The door was open, so the mouse ran out of the house. Did the cat do that too? The cat did not. So what do you think the men called the cat then? Yes. Now they say it's a good cat.

Read   Have children read the book softly or silently on their own. As necessary, use appropriate prompts from page 25 to support readers. Make notes about any processing difficulties children have to help you choose teaching points later.

Respond   Invite children to tell and/or write an alternate ending for the story—one in which the cat follows the mouse out of the house.

Revisit   Use your observation notes to select teaching points that will be the most helpful. For example:

- using information from pictures to confirm what the text says

- recognizing the purposes of exclamation points

- recognizing and understanding words that tell where things happen in relation to objects (*under, over, on, across, out*)

Optional Extensions   **Cooperative Writing** Children work together to make a list of the things the cat did that made the men call it a bad cat and a list of the things it did that made them call it a good cat. They can add to the second list other things the cat might have done to be called a good cat.

Home Connection

If possible, allow children to take *The Good Bad Cat* home to read aloud. Suggest that after they read, they talk with family members about the art work in this book and what their favorite pictures were.

Informal Assessment

Observing Readers Ask children to read three pages of the book aloud for you. Note how quickly and easily they recognize and read high-frequency words such as *good, bad, saw, out, so, under.*

Book 7

Emergent

Teaching Tip

For some children, this story will immediately bring to mind *Goldilocks and the Three Bears*. You might wish to read aloud this classic, particularly to those children for whom it might not be familiar.

Home Connection

Send *A Mosquito Buzzed* home for children to enjoy with someone there. Ask them to talk about how people in their families would get rid of a mosquito.

Informal Assessment

Observing Readers Sometimes a chuckle can tell you a lot about how an individual reader is enjoying a funny story. Watch for signs of enjoyment as children read.

A Mosquito Buzzed

by Kana Riley; illustrated by Daniel Moreton

Book Features

A humorous fantasy with decorative type treatment and sound words

SMALL-GROUP INSTRUCTION

Introduce
Read aloud the cover and title page. Point out the word *mosquito*, and ask children what sound a mosquito makes. Talk with children about what it's like to have a mosquito buzzing in your ears when you're trying to sleep and how annoying that can be. Explain that in this story a family of bears had that problem. Papa Bear got rid of the mosquito by breaking a window! Browse through a few pages, following the *Buzzzz* across them. You may wish to make the following points, emphasizing the words in italics.

- (pp. 2–3) Baby Bear was *sleeping*. *Snore, snore, snore*. Say *snore*. What letter will it begin with? Find *snore* on the page. Now a mosquito buzzed near Baby's ear. What sound did the mosquito make? (*Buzz, buzz, buzz*) Put your finger under the words.
- (pp. 4–5) *Slap!* went Baby Bear. Say *Slap!* Find the word on the page. *Slap!* tells what Baby Bear did and also the sound he made.
- (pp. 12–13) Papa Bear had a tennis racket. "I'll get that mosquito," he said. What do you think he did?
- (pp. 14–16) *Crash!* went the *window*. Say and find the word *Crash!* The mosquito went *out* the *window*. Now look at page 16. Did the bears solve their problem? Why not?

Read
Have children read the book softly or silently. Help as necessary. See page 25 for prompts. Make notes about any processing difficulties children have to help you select teaching points for Revisit.

Respond
Ask children what they think of Papa Bear's "solution" to the problem. How would they have solved it? Then have volunteers choose favorite pages to read with expression.

Revisit
Use your notes to select teaching points that address children's needs. For example:

- using information from pictures to support meaning and to predict (Baby slapping the mosquito; Papa with the tennis racket)
- using familiar word parts to read longer words (*buzzed, sleeping*)
- rereading to correct an error

Optional Extensions
Shared Writing Encourage children to think of another funny way to get rid of a mosquito. Then collaborate to write directions. Include *Buzzzzz* and other sound words.

Drama As a narrator reads aloud, three other children can act out the story.

The Secret Friend

by Marcia Vaughan; illustrated by John Sandford

Book 8

Emergent

Book Features

Predictable text,
some of it in letter format

SMALL-GROUP INSTRUCTION

Introduce
Read the title and the names of the author and illustrator. Discuss the animals on the cover, pointing out that each animal gets a letter from a secret friend. None of them can figure out who that friend might be. The animals finally discover that Snake is the secret friend who has been sending the letters. In the end, Snake gets a letter of his own—from his five new friends. Highlight important language patterns, words, and pictures as you introduce the book to children.

- (pp. 2–3) One day *Squirrel* found a letter on his tree. The letter was from someone who liked him. It was signed *XXXOOO*, which means hugs and kisses. There was no name on the letter, but it was signed Your *Secret* Friend and (Can you *guess* who?).

- (pp. 4–5) Squirrel said to Fox, "Is this letter from you?" The letter wasn't from Fox, but she had gotten one just like Squirrel's. Say *one. One* begins with *o*. Find the word *one*.

- (pp. 6–11) The animals went to *Bear, Moose,* and *Owl,* looking for the secret friend who sent the letters. They asked, "Are these letters from you?" Say *are*. It begins with an *a*. Find it. Each animal got the same letter from a secret friend, but they didn't know who the secret friend was.

- (pp. 12–13) The animals *thought*, "Who can it be?" Say *who*. It begins with *wh*. Find it. Snake cried, "Surprise! Your secret friend is me!"

- (pp. 14–16) The very next day Snake found a letter on his tree. Can you guess who sent the letter? Read to find out who sent Snake a letter.

Read
Have children read the story softly or silently on their own. Use appropriate prompts from page 25 as necessary to support readers. Make notes to help you select important teaching points after the reading.

Respond
Discuss with the group whether they were surprised to find out who the secret friend was. If they received a letter from a secret friend, how would they go about finding out who had sent it?

Revisit
Use your notes to select helpful teaching points. Some suggestions:
- using letters or word parts to solve words
- using pictures to check when words don't look or sound right
- reading dialogue with fluency and expression
- reading the text of a friendly letter and understanding the format

Optional Extensions
Writing Invite children to write about things they like to do with their friends.
Reading Encourage children to partner-read the book, with one child reading the narrative and the other reading the letters.

Classroom Management Tip

Use a book that a child has previously read when conducting an oral reading check. This will ensure that the child is reading for meaning. Look at children's book logs to select an appropriate book.

Teaching Tip

The words set in quotation marks on page 12 may be interpreted by some readers as dialogue. Mention that quotation marks are sometimes used to indicate what characters are thinking, as is the case on page 12. Readers should use the words before and after the quotation marks to determine whether something is being spoken or thought.

Home Connection

Children can take *The Secret Friend* home and read it to a family member or friend. Together, they might write a letter that Snake sends back to one of the characters in the book.

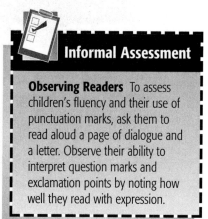

Informal Assessment

Observing Readers To assess children's fluency and their use of punctuation marks, ask them to read aloud a page of dialogue and a letter. Observe their ability to interpret question marks and exclamation points by noting how well they read with expression.

Book 9

Emergent

Smile, Baby!

by Deborah Eaton; illustrated by Melissa Sweet

Book Features

Humorous, episodic structure, with pictures that tell part of the story

SMALL-GROUP INSTRUCTION

Teaching Tip

Encourage children who are whisper-reading to try reading a few pages silently as well. Watch for signs that children need support, such as hesitation in the middle of a sentence or breaks in their concentration, asking them to read quietly aloud to you as necessary.

Home Connection

Encourage children to read *Smile, Baby!* at home to family members. Suggest that after they read, they talk with family members about ways in which the story reminds them of their own families.

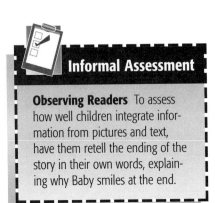

Informal Assessment

Observing Readers To assess how well children integrate information from pictures and text, have them retell the ending of the story in their own words, explaining why Baby smiles at the end.

Introduce Read the title and the author's and illustrator's names. Ask children if they have ever tried to take a family picture. What happened? Tell them that this is a funny story about a family that's trying to get Baby to smile for a picture. Using the characters' names, explain that Poppy, Mommy, Rosa, Carlos, and even Rags the dog all try different ways to make Baby smile. Show the characters in the pictures as you say their names. Then guide children through the book, helping them notice important information in its words, pictures, story events, and language. Some suggestions follow.

- (pp. 2–3) There's the whole family. Poppy wanted to take a picture of *everybody*. He said, "Smile!"
- (pp. 4–5) Almost everybody smiled—Mommy, Rosa, Carlos, and Rags, too. But not Baby.
- (pp. 6–7) Poppy said, "Peek-a-boo! Peek-a-boo!" to make Baby smile. Everybody else smiled at Poppy. But not Baby.
- (pp. 8–10) Mommy said, "Booga, booga, booga!" Say *booga, booga, booga*. What letter does it start with? Find those three *boogas*. Poppy said, "Peek-a-boo! Peek-a-boo!" Rosa and Carlos and Rags smiled. But not Baby.
- (pp. 11–15) Rosa said, "Watch the birdie!" to try to make Baby smile. Say *watch*. What letter will you see first? Find *watch*. Carlos and Rags tried dancing to make Baby smile. Mommy and Poppy kept on saying, "Booga, booga, booga!" and "Peek-a-boo!" Everybody tried to make Baby smile! Then Poppy said, "Peek-a-YIKES!" Say *peek-a-yikes* and find it. And what did Baby do? You can read the whole book to find out.

Read Have children read quietly or silently. Intervene when necessary, choosing appropriate prompts (see page 25) to help children process the text. Make notes to help you select teaching opportunities after the reading.

Respond Ask children if they expected Baby to smile. Why? Then ask children to read aloud the parts of the story they thought were the funniest.

Revisit Use your notes to select helpful teaching points. Possibilities include:
- understanding the story's structure and humor
- reading dialogue and keeping track of which character is speaking
- using text and pictures together to make sense of the story events

Put *Smile, Baby!* in the browsing basket for rereading later.

Optional Extensions **Writing** Invite partners to write a few sentences telling why Baby smiles at the end of the story. As necessary, suggest that they describe, in their own words, what happens on page 15 and why it makes Baby smile.

Drama Encourage children to each choose a character and then act out the story together. One child can be the narrator.

Early

The information on this page is meant to help you select appropriately leveled texts for children to develop effective reading behaviors. The descriptions are broad, and you should expect some overlap between Early and other reading stages. To identify each child's approximate reading stage and to provide the child with appropriate books, use your observation notes and the oral reading checks you have recorded for that child.

Most Early readers

▸ are able to read most books independently when the texts are matched to their control of reading behaviors and when the books have been introduced by the teacher

▸ can use more than one strategy or problem-solving technique to figure out an unfamiliar word or meaning

▸ will stop as they read when they notice that something is wrong with the sounds of words or phrases or with their appearance or meaning—and then reread to correct

▸ are able to recognize a growing number of high-frequency words

▸ can apply problem-solving strategies to different kinds of texts

Children who exhibit many but not necessarily all of the above behaviors should be able to successfully process and yet be appropriately challenged by books in an Early group.

Books suitable for Early readers contain ideas and concepts that are a bit more involved than in earlier stages, and the stories may develop over a longer time span. They represent a variety of genres, such as directions, legends, folktales, humor and information. The vocabulary gradually becomes more challenging and the sentences grow in length and complexity. They still provide pictures on most pages to support the text. But the pictures do not always illustrate every aspect of the text, so readers are required to pay closer attention to details in the print. Books in this stage are

The Three Billy Goats Gruff

Washing the Dog

The Crazy Quilt

How to Make a Mud Pie

Lift the Sky Up

The Mystery of the Missing Red Mitten

Coaching to Problem-Solve

The **Early** reader exhibits more independence and more control of reading behaviors. As you coach these children during their reading, use your anecdotal records to note particular strategies they use effectively, and look for ways to support specific behaviors that will move them toward fluency at each stage. Here are a few coaching statements or prompts that may be helpful for these readers.

► To help readers use visual cues to read unfamiliar words:
  Do you see a part of the word you know?

► To ensure that readers use all sources of information:
  I notice that you said _____. That makes sense, but does it look right? Why not?

► To encourage the use of self-checking behaviors:
  Do you know the tricky part? What made you stop?

► To develop smooth, fluent phrasing:
  Try saying that as if you were talking.

Note: *For a comprehensive discussion of coaching statements or prompts to guide the reading and for a more extensive list of leveled books for early readers, see* Guided Reading: Good First Teaching for All Children, *by Irene C. Fountas and Gay Su Pinnell, published by Heinemann.*

Book 10

Early

Teaching Tip

If you keep special collections of easy-to-read old tales and fables in browsing boxes or baskets, add this book and other versions of it to the collection. Because these books have familiar story lines and storybook language, as well as appealing art, they are popular with many children.

Home Connection

Suggest that children take *The Three Billy Goats Gruff* home to read aloud with family members. When they return to class, ask them how they and their families enjoyed reading this old tale together and if anyone had read or heard it before. If possible, allow children to check out different versions of this tale from the classroom or school library.

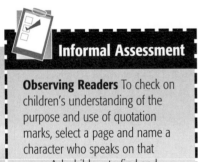

Informal Assessment

Observing Readers To check on children's understanding of the purpose and use of quotation marks, select a page and name a character who speaks on that page. Ask children to find and read the exact words the character says.

The Three Billy Goats Gruff

retold by Susan McCloskey;
illustrated by Patricia Beling Murphy

Book Features

A familiar tale, retold in dialogue and narration

SMALL-GROUP INSTRUCTION

Introduce Read the cover aloud. Tell children that they may have heard this story before and that now they will be able to read it. Explain that in this story three goat brothers, whose last name is Gruff, are hungry and want to eat some grass. But a mean man, called a troll, tries to stop each goat on a bridge. Little and Middle Billy Goat trick the troll into waiting for their big brother. When Big Billy Goat comes to the bridge, he knocks the troll off. Then the three goats get the yummy grass. Guide children through the book, helping them notice important information in its pictures, story, language, and words.

- (pp. 2–5) *Once upon a time*. Get a good look at those four words. The three Billy Goats Gruff were *hungry* and had to *cross* a *bridge* to get some grass. *Trip-trap, trip-trap* was the sound the goats' hooves made on the bridge. Say *Trip-trap, trip-trap* and get a look at those words.

- (pp. 6–11) When Little (Middle) Billy Goat tried to cross the bridge, the troll said, "Hey, I'm going to eat you up." Say *Hey*. What letter do you expect to see first? Find it. But Little (Middle) Billy Goat told the troll to wait for his big brother and to "Eat him *instead*." Say *instead*. What letter will it start with? Find it.

- (pp. 12–16) The trip-trap sound Big Billy Goat made was very loud. This Billy Goat was so big that when the troll said, "I'm going to eat you up," he bumped the troll off the bridge. Do you think that the goats' idea about getting past the troll was a good one? The grass was *yummy. Yummy* means it tasted good.

Read Have children read this book softly or silently. Support them as necessary (see prompts on page 33), making notes about any processing difficulties they have to help you select important teaching points later.

Respond Encourage discussion about the characters and events in this tale, inviting comparisons with other tales children know, such as *The Three Little Pigs*.

Revisit Use your observation notes as you choose the teaching points that will be most helpful. For example:

- using more than one source of information for checking new words
- understanding that emphasis and feeling can be shown by punctuation and special uses of print
- recognizing that pictures can tell part of a story when the words don't

Optional Extensions **Writing** Work with children to make a story map on a chart that they can use as a prompt when they want to retell this story.

Washing the Dog

by Peter Sloan and Sheryl Sloan

Book Features

Simple step-by-step directions, accompanied by photographs

SMALL-GROUP INSTRUCTION

Introduce Read aloud the title and authors' names. Invite children who have ever tried to wash a dog to tell what that was like. Explain that in this book a boy and a girl tell, in order, all the things you should do when you wash your dog. Guide children through the book, helping them notice important information in the text and photographs and pointing out particular features of written directions. Invite them to comment as well. Some suggestions follow.

- (p. 2) To wash a dog, you need lots of things. Look at the picture and find some of the things you need. See the large tub? The girl and boy will put some warm water in this tub.

- (p. 3) Directions often use words like *First* and *Next* at the beginning of sentences. This page tells what to do *First*. Say *First*. What letter do you expect to see at the beginning? Find *First* and take a look at it.

- (pp. 4–5) These pages tell what to do *Next. Next* you should put your dog in the tub and talk *nicely* to it. Say *nicely*. Then you should pour warm water over your dog.

- (p. 6) In this part, they say to rub soap over the dog's fur *when* the dog is wet. Say *when*. What two letters do you expect to see first? Find *when*.

- (p. 7) In this picture they are rinsing the dog. What does *rinse* mean?

- (p. 8) *Finally*, they tell you to dry the dog. Say *Finally*. It begins with *f*. Find it. Now read the book to find out what you should do to wash a dog.

Read Have children read the book softly or silently. Intervene as necessary, using prompts such as those on page 33. Make notes about any processing difficulties children have to help you select teaching points after reading.

Respond Invite children to compare *Washing the Dog* to other nonfiction books they have read, such as *Things I Can Do* and *At the Supermarket*. Discuss what makes directions different from other kinds of nonfiction, and have children find examples in the book.

Revisit Use your notes to select important teaching points. For example:
- understanding the importance of sequence words in directions
- using pictures to confirm meaning
- checking what looks right and what makes sense

Optional Extensions **Shared Writing** Brainstorm simple activities that children know how to do. Work with the group to select one activity and write directions for it.

Reading One child can read *Washing the Dog* aloud while others pantomime. They can do the same with the directions from Shared Writing.

Teaching Tip

Provide support for children who may have trouble understanding the selection by reminding them to use the photographs to check what they read.

🏠 Home Connection

Invite children to share *Washing the Dog* with family members. Suggest that they ask older family members about what kinds of written directions they use (recipes, instruction manuals, etc.) and why they use them. They might like to find examples around the house.

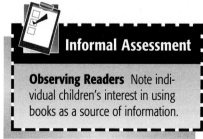

Informal Assessment

Observing Readers Note individual children's interest in using books as a source of information.

Book 12

Early

Classroom Management Tip

Encourage children to return to books they have already read successfully. This will build their confidence as they engage in the behavior of a good reader.

Home Connection

Children can take *The Crazy Quilt* home to read to family members. Have children notice whether their families can predict what Tanya is going to do with all the family clothing.

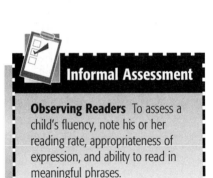

Informal Assessment

Observing Readers To assess a child's fluency, note his or her reading rate, appropriateness of expression, and ability to read in meaningful phrases.

The Crazy Quilt

by Kristin Avery; illustrated by David McPhail

Book Features
Humorous story with repetitive language

SMALL-GROUP INSTRUCTION

Introduce Read aloud the title and the author's and illustrator's names. Have children look at the title page and describe what they see. In this story Tanya finds a crazy quilt. Explain that a crazy quilt is a type of blanket made from patches of different clothes of all shapes, colors, sizes, and patterns. After Tanya's mother tells her the story of the crazy quilt, Tanya decides to make a quilt of her own. Guide children through the book, helping them notice important information in its language, pictures, story, or words.

- (pp. 2–3) Tanya found a *quilt.* Her mother told her it was a *crazy quilt* because it was made from *favorite clothes.* What are *favorite* clothes?

- (pp. 4–9) The favorite clothes belonged to Tanya's older relatives. Tanya asks about the *gray (blue, red)* spot, and her mother tells her that it came from *Uncle's favorite coat (Grandpa's favorite shirt, Grandma's favorite skirt).* Look at the pictures in the thought balloons. They show each relative that Tanya's mother is talking about.

- (pp. 10–13) After Tanya hears about the crazy quilt, she has an *idea.* Say *idea.* What letter does it start with? Point to *idea.* Tanya decides to get her *brother's shirt (sister's skirt, father's tie, mother's scarf).* What do you think Tanya will do with these things?

- (pp. 14–16) The *next morning*, Tanya's family is looking for their missing clothes. Where are their clothes? Tanya has made her own crazy quilt using her family's favorite clothes!

Read Invite children to read softly or silently on their own. Choose appropriate prompts (see page 33) to support their reading when necessary. Make notes about any processing difficulties children may have to plan later instruction.

Respond Ask children how they think Tanya felt about the crazy quilt she made. How would they have felt if their favorite clothing had been used for a crazy quilt?

Revisit Choose important teaching points based on your notes. For example:

- checking for what looks right and makes sense
- recognizing word categories such as clothing words and family words
- reading contractions with *is* (*What's, It's, That's, Where's*)
- reading dialogue smoothly and with expression

Optional Extensions **Writing** Have children imagine that they are going to make their own crazy quilts using the favorite clothing of their own family members. Ask them to tell where each piece of clothing comes from and what it looks like, using this pattern: *I found my _____.*

Rereading Encourage children to reread this book for independent reading.

How to Make a Mud Pie

by Deborah Eaton; illustrated by Nadine Bernard Westcott

Book 13

Early

Book Features

Humorous directions for how to make something familiar to most children

SMALL-GROUP INSTRUCTION

Introduce Read the title and the author's and illustrator's names. Invite children to tell what they know about making mud pies. Explain that the boy in the yellow shirt on page 2 is making a mud pie and that the other boy is his brother. At the end, the children surprise their mother and father and dog with mud pies. Then they make more mud pies with their friends—because everybody loves mud pie! Help children notice important information in its pictures, story, language, or words as you lead them through the book.

- (pp. 2–5) The directions say it's easy to make a mud pie. *First* you find some good dirt. Say *First*. What letter does it begin with? Find it. "Fill some pans with water. Dump the water on the dirt." *Dump* means to put it in all at once, just like the boy is doing. On page 5, the boy is mixing the mud with a spoon. The directions say to mix it some more, using *your fingers and your toes.*

- (pp. 6–9) Now put in some rocks to make it *crunchy* and some fat, *wiggly worms.* Say *crunchy* (*wiggly worms*) and find that. What does the boy do?

- (pp. 10–12) The directions say to make the mud *gooey.* What does *gooey* mean? After the boys pat the mud, where do they put it? When the pie is done, what do the boys do with it? *Yum, yum, yum!* Who loves mud pie?

Read Have children read the whole book softly or silently. As necessary, intervene to support readers. (See page 33.) Make notes about any processing difficulties children have to help you select teaching points later.

Respond Encourage children to retell in their own words the directions for mud pies. Ask them to show the picture for the part of the story they thought was the funniest and to tell why they thought so.

Revisit Use your observation notes to choose the important teaching points that will be the most helpful. For example:

- noticing the language structure of directions or commands
- recognizing that an author's use of descriptive words such as *crunchy, wiggly,* or *gooey,* aids understanding and can make stories more interesting

Optional Extensions **Independent Writing** Provide large index cards, and encourage children to write and illustrate their own recipes for mud pies or sand cakes.

Rereading Encourage groups to reread the book chorally as volunteers pantomime the actions.

Classroom Management Tip

On a regular basis, review the independent activity options with children to make sure they understand the routines. Each time, reinforce that they are expected to carry out these activities as quietly and independently as possible, allowing you to pay full attention to the group that is reading.

 Home Connection

Allow children to take *How to Make a Mud Pie* home to read aloud. Children can ask their family members to share funny experiences they remember about making something.

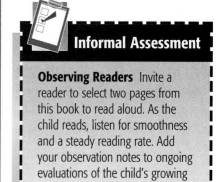 **Informal Assessment**

Observing Readers Invite a reader to select two pages from this book to read aloud. As the child reads, listen for smoothness and a steady reading rate. Add your observation notes to ongoing evaluations of the child's growing fluency.

Book 14

Early

Lift the Sky Up

retold by Richard Vaughan; illustrated by Robin Moore

Book Features

A legend told in simple language with art that provides a cultural connection to the text

SMALL-GROUP INSTRUCTION

Teaching Tip

To provide motivation for independent reading, suggest that children reread *Lift the Sky Up* in order to retell it to a friend.

FYI

Point out to children that long ago, many Native American groups had no written language. The Native Americans taught their children through stories, and these stories were passed down to other children over the years. That is how many of the Native American stories are known today.

Home Connection

Children can take *Lift the Sky Up* home to read to family members. Suggest that children ask their families if they know any legends or stories about how things came to be. They can share these stories with the group when they return the books.

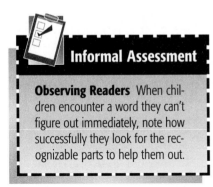

Informal Assessment

Observing Readers When children encounter a word they can't figure out immediately, note how successfully they look for the recognizable parts to help them out.

Introduce Read the cover. This book is a special kind of folktale that explains why things happened. The Snohomish people made up this legend to explain how the Big Dipper came to be in the sky. Display page 16, pointing out that the Big Dipper is a group of stars that looks like a cup with a long handle. In this legend, the sky was so low the people decided to lift it up. Before they could begin, though, three boys and four deer ran up into the sky. When the sky was lifted, the boys and the deer couldn't get down. They became the stars that form the Big Dipper. Introduce the book to children, drawing their attention to important information in its language, pictures, story, or words.

- (pp. 2–3) The story begins, like many folktales or legends, with the words *Once upon a time*. The *sky* was very *low*. The sky was so low that people *bumped* their heads on it. Animals *jumped* into the sky to hide.

- (pp. 4–9) But people got tired of bumping their heads on the sky. People got tired of *chasing* animals into the sky. The people decided that they would use *long poles* to lift the sky up.

- (pp. 10–16) As the sky was falling asleep, three boys chased four *deer* into the sky. The boys and the deer were still in the sky when the people lifted the sky up. The last two words on page 12 are in dark print, and the last word is in capital letters to show that each word is read a little louder than the one before it. The people lifted the sky so *high* that the boys and the deer couldn't get down. The boys and the deer turned into *twinkling stars*. The last words on page 16 tell the name of the group of stars, the *Big Dipper*.

Read Have children read the book silently. Intervene with appropriate prompts from page 33 as necessary. Make notes about any processing difficulties children have to help you select important teaching points later.

Respond Encourage the group to create a cooperative story map. Provide a story-map form and have children write down the setting, characters, and problem and solution. Using the story map, they can retell the story in their own words.

Revisit Use your notes to help you choose important teaching points. For example:

- integrating more than one source of information to figure out new words
- recognizing opposites (*low/high, day/night, up/down*)
- recognizing sequence of events

Optional Extensions **Shared Writing** Encourage children to think of other explanations for how the Big Dipper came to be in the sky. Work together to write a group legend.

Drama A narrator can reread the story aloud as other children act it out.

The Mystery of the Missing Red Mitten

story and pictures by Steven Kellogg

Book 15
Early

Book Features

A mystery told completely in dialogue; thought balloons show possible solutions

SMALL-GROUP INSTRUCTION

Introduce   Read the cover aloud. Explain what a *mystery* is and talk with children about any other mysteries they've read. Tell them that in this mystery, Annie searches for her lost red mitten with her dog, Oscar. As she searches, she imagines what could have happened to the mitten. Show children the thought balloon on page 10, which shows something Annie imagines. As in most mysteries, there is a surprise at the end that tells how the mystery is solved. Guide children through the book, helping them notice important information in the text and pictures and engaging them in conversation.

- (pp. 6–7) Annie is talking to her dog, *Oscar*. Say *Oscar*. Annie tells Oscar that she has lost her other mitten. She is going to *search* for it. *Search* means to look for something that is lost.
- (pp. 8–9) *Here's* Ralph's boot, but *there's* no mitten. Say *Here's*. What letter would you expect to see first? Find *Here's*. It means "Here is."
- (pp. 10–11) The picture in the balloon shows what Annie imagines—Oscar as a *bloodhound*. A bloodhound is a kind of dog with a very good sense of smell. If Oscar were a bloodhound, he could track down Annie's mitten.
- (pp. 12, 18–19) The pictures in the balloons show other things that Annie imagines: mice are using her mitten as a *sleeping bag*; a *hawk* took it.
- (p. 21) Miss Seltzer tells Annie to look in the garden where she was making *snow angels*. Can you find the snow angels in the picture?
- (pp. 23–27) Annie imagines what would happen if she *planted* her other mitten. We know she is imagining these things because of the balloons.
- What do you think really happened? How was the mystery solved?

Read   Have children read the book softly or silently to find the answer to the mystery. If necessary, intervene, using prompts from page 33. Make notes to help you select teaching points for Revisit.

Respond   Ask children if they would recommend *The Mystery of the Missing Red Mitten* to others. What would they like to tell someone about this book?

Revisit   Use your notes to select important teaching points. For example:
- using familiar word parts to figure out new words
- distinguishing between real and imaginary events
- reading contractions (*I'm, I'll, Here's, there's, I'd, What's*)
- using text clues and personal experience to draw conclusions

Optional Extensions   **Writing** Ask children to imagine some other things that could have happened to the red mitten. Have them draw their ideas in thought balloons and write sentences to go with their drawings.

Teaching Tip

Steven Kellogg's style in this book is to use dialogue without quotation marks and without saying "he/she said." Help children as necessary to use context to figure out who is speaking in the scenes involving Annie and Miss Seltzer (pages 21, 29, 30–32).

Home Connection

Encourage children to take *The Mystery of the Missing Red Mitten* home to read with family members. Suggest that they ask family members to share their own experiences with looking for lost items and finding them in surprising places.

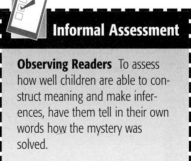

Informal Assessment

Observing Readers To assess how well children are able to construct meaning and make inferences, have them tell in their own words how the mystery was solved.

LITTLE READERS

Fluent

The information on this page is meant to help you select appropriately leveled texts for children to develop effective reading behaviors. The descriptions are broad, and you should expect some overlap between Fluent and other reading stages. To identify each child's approximate reading stage and to provide the child with appropriate books, use your observation notes and the oral reading checks you have recorded for that child.

Most Fluent readers

- ▸ are able to focus on longer texts
- ▸ can identify sources of information related to the texts they are reading and make use of more than one to solve a problem
- ▸ can figure out most unfamiliar words with little hesitation
- ▸ can read many texts with growing smoothness and phrasing
- ▸ self-check more consistently and automatically as they read

Children who exhibit many but not necessarily all of the above behaviors should be able to successfully process and yet be appropriately challenged by books in a Fluent group.

Books suitable for Fluent readers are longer and usually include more than one incident or event. Some use paragraphs to reflect more than one idea per page, and the longer ones may be divided into chapters. They continue to present themes familiar to children and of high interest to them, although some of the nonfiction books extend into areas that may not be from children's own experiences. Their range and complexity of vocabulary and language structures continue to increase. Some may deal with both present events and events recalled from the past. They carry more detailed descriptions, and a wider variety of style in the illustrations is represented. Books in this stage are

Nobody Listens to Andrew	Bears, Bears, Bears
Bookstore Cat	Happy Birthday, Danny and the Dinosaur!
Digby	Henry and Mudge: The First Book
Mrs. Murphy's Bears	Henry and Mudge Get the Cold Shivers
Who Lives Here?	Dogs at Work
The Lost Sheep	Addie's Bad Day
Anansi's Narrow Waist	The Grandma Mix-up

Coaching to Problem-Solve

Fluent readers are able to read silently with effective strategies, so it may be necessary to ask them to read a page or a passage aloud to check their progress. You can judge when to intervene if you carefully watch these readers as they problem-solve. Does the reader stop or seem to lose concentration? Here are some coaching statements that can help readers as they grow in confidence and competence.

▶ To encourage readers to use what they know about language structures:
  What do you notice about how that sounds? Does it sound right?

▶ To foster the ability to recognize an error while reading:
  I like the way you stopped and reread to find your mistake.

▶ To encourage readers to predict meaning from syntax:
  Why can't _____ be right? What would sound right?

▶ To encourage the use of all sources of information:
  Look at the picture. Does it help you?

Note: *For a comprehensive discussion of coaching statements, or prompts, to guide the reading and for a more extensive list of leveled books for early readers, see* Guided Reading: Good First Teaching for All Children, *by Irene C. Fountas and Gay Su Pinnell, published by Heinemann.*

Book 16

Fluent

Nobody Listens to Andrew

by Elizabeth Guilfoile; pictures by Dora Leder

Book Features

Humorous fiction
with repeated language patterns

FYI

Reinforce safety with animals by pointing out that the story about Andrew and the bear is a make-believe story and that in real life bears and all other wild animals should not be approached or handled. Only people who are trained to work with animals, such as zookeepers or veterinarians, should go near them.

Home Connection

If possible, allow children to take *Nobody Listens to Andrew* home to read aloud. Suggest that they invite an older family member to read alternate pages of the book aloud with them as the rest of the family listens.

Informal Assessment

Observing Readers To assess children's growth in fluency, have them choose and read aloud a familiar passage. Make notes on how confidently and quickly they read and whether they are reading in phrases. Compare these notes to other, earlier notes you have made on their fluency.

SMALL-GROUP INSTRUCTION

Introduce Tell children the title, author, and illustrator. Talk about times when children had something important to say, but nobody would listen. Explain that in this story Andrew tries to tell Mother, Daddy, Ruthy, Bobby, and Mr. Neighbor that he just saw something upstairs in his bed on the sun porch and it was black. But each person he talks to is too busy to listen. Finally, Andrew tells them that what he saw was a bear. Invite children to look at the picture on pages 22–23 to see the excitement Andrew has caused. The following points about words, phrases, language patterns, and meanings emphasize important information in the story that may be helpful.

- (pp. 4–7) Andrew tries to tell Mother (Daddy) about what he saw, but she (he) must pay Mrs. Cleaner (cut the grass).

- (pp. 8–15) As Andrew tries to tell other people about what he saw, they each tell Andrew what she or he must do "before dark." So nobody listens. Then Andrew tells everyone, "There is a bear upstairs in my bed."

- (pp. 16–23) "Call the police (fire department, zoo, dog catcher)," everybody said. All the people called came to Andrew's house. Say *Zoom, Zing, Whoosh, Swish*. Those are the words that match the sounds the people made as they drove up to Andrew's house.

- (pp. 24–32) Everybody ran upstairs and saw that there really was a bear in Andrew's room. The man from the zoo said, "It is dry in the woods. The bears are *thirsty*. They are looking for water." Say *thirsty*. What two letters do you expect it to start with? Find it. You can read on your own to find out where they took the bear.

Read Have children read the whole book softly or silently. If they hesitate, coach them with appropriate prompts. (See page 41.) Make notes on any difficulties children may have to help you choose important teaching points later.

Respond Ask children what they would have done if they had been Andrew.

Revisit The observation notes you took during reading should help you choose important teaching points, such as:

- self-checking by rereading for more sources of information
- noting changes in repeated language patterns
- reading dialogue with appropriate intonation and stress

Optional Extensions **Independent Writing** Have children make a list of all the people Andrew told about what he saw. Ask them to write the list in the order in which Andrew talked to them. They can use their lists to help them retell the story.

Bookstore Cat

by Cindy Wheeler

Book Features

Humorous story
with strong cause-effect structure;
entertaining central character

Book 17
Fluent

SMALL-GROUP INSTRUCTION

Introduce   Read the cover to children, and point out Mulligan. Tell children that in this story the author says Mulligan has many jobs. But the pictures show that Mulligan mostly plays and looks out the window. One day a pigeon gets into the bookstore, and Mulligan tries to catch it. But he ends up catching a stuffed parrot instead. Suggestions follow for guiding children through important aspects of the book and inviting conversation.

- (pp. 4–11) Here's Mulligan, in the bookstore. Say *Mulligan* and get a good look at the word. The author says that Mulligan is great at *entertaining customers*. To *entertain* means to have others pay attention to you, usually because you are doing something funny or interesting.

- (pp. 12–15) Mulligan was *curious* about the bookseller's new sign, so he *kept an eye on it*. That means he watched it closely. The sign said "Story Hour Today," and lots of people were coming to the store. But Mulligan didn't *notice* how busy the store was because he had spotted a pigeon.

- (pp. 16–21) When the pigeon followed a customer into the store, Mulligan *sprang* into action. The picture shows what *sprang* means.

- (pp. 22–25) There's the pigeon, next to a funny-looking bird. That's a stuffed parrot, isn't it? But Mulligan thinks there are TWO live birds in the store now. So he *pounced*, or jumped quickly, to try to catch them.

- (pp. 26–32) When all was quiet, Mulligan had one bird; the bookseller had the other. Mulligan is very pleased with himself and purrs, "Well done." Isn't it lucky for the pigeon that Mulligan got the stuffed parrot and not the pigeon? *Don't you think* every bookstore needs a cat like Mulligan?

Read   Have children read the book silently. As necessary, coach them with appropriate prompts from page 41. Make notes about any processing difficulties they may have to help you choose important teaching points later in the lesson.

Respond   Talk about what parts of the story children thought were funniest. Invite them to write their ideas in their journals.

Revisit   Use your notes to choose helpful teaching points. Some possibilities:
- recognizing sequence of events and cause-effect relationships
- integrating several sources of information to understand a character
- discovering that word choice, language structure, and punctuation all work together to create excitement and humor (see page 25 in particular)

Optional Extensions   **Writing** Children can write about Mulligan visiting school for a day.

Rereading Partners can reread this story to each other, listening for excitement and humor in each other's voices.

Teaching Tip

English learners may need extra help with the phrases *kept an eye on*, *sprang into action*, and *don't you think*. Introduce the phrases and explain their meanings. Then help children find them on pages 13, 21, and 32, respectively.

Home Connection

Children will enjoy sharing *Bookstore Cat* with their families. Suggest that they talk about why the customers like Mulligan, even though he creates such a mess.

Informal Assessment

Observing Readers To assess how well children understand character development and cause-effect relationships, ask them to retell the story. Note whether they understand the interaction between the pictures and the text and how together these elements give readers a complete picture of what Mulligan is like and what he does.

Book 18

Fluent

Digby

by Barbara Shook Hazen; pictures by Barbara J. Phillips-Duke

Teaching Tip

You may want to point out to children before they read that while this story gives the exact words of the brother and the sister as they talk to one another, their words are not set off by quotation marks. Explain that the pictures and the language pattern of questions from the brother and answers from the sister will help them understand who is speaking.

Home Connection

Allow children to take *Digby* home to read aloud. Suggest that parents or other grown-up family members could tell them about how they, the children, learned to walk, play catch, or do other things and who helped them learn how.

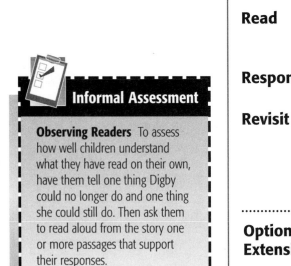

Informal Assessment

Observing Readers To assess how well children understand what they have read on their own, have them tell one thing Digby could no longer do and one thing she could still do. Then ask them to read aloud from the story one or more passages that support their responses.

SMALL-GROUP INSTRUCTION

Introduce   Read the title and the author's and illustrator's names. Engage children in a dialogue about pets. Explain that this story is a conversation. A girl and her little brother talk to each other about Digby, their family dog. Digby is getting old and can't do some things anymore. The sister tells her brother about the things she remembers doing with Digby when she was little, and what the dog can still do. Help children focus on important information in the book's pictures, story, language, or words as you lead them through it.

- (pp. 5–11) The little brother tries to get Digby to run and catch the ball. When his sister says Digby is too old to play catch, her brother asks, "How do you *know*?" "Because I am older and I know more," she answers.
- (pp. 12–21) The sister says Digby was "here before I was *born*." She shows a picture of Digby and herself when she was a baby and tells about what Digby helped her *learn* to do. Say *born* (*learn*). What letter will you see first? Find the word.
- (pp. 22–27) The sister reminds her brother that Digby can't jump now, and he asks what Digby can do now. She tells some things that Digby is better at now, such as waiting, watching, and *understanding*. That means Digby knows more about what's going on. Say *understanding* and clap the parts.
- (pp. 28–32) The girl says she can show her brother how to catch like Digby did. She also says, "*You'll* have to *practice* a lot to be as good as I am." Say *You'll* (*practice*). What letter do you expect the word to start with? The two children ask Digby to come along and watch them play. Do you think that makes Digby happy?

Read   Have children read the whole book softly or silently. Intervene with prompts when necessary to support readers. (See page 41.) Make notes on any difficulties children may have to help you decide teaching points to focus on later.

Respond   Encourage readers to discuss how the children in the story feel about their dog Digby and how they, the readers, feel about Digby too.

Revisit   The observation notes you made during the reading can help you choose teaching points, such as the following, which you can to use now:

- recognizing when words or phrases don't sound right or make sense
- using different word forms to understand whether the story is talking about the past or the present (*is, am, can, was, did*)

Optional Extensions   **Cooperative Writing** Ask the group to write a conversation between two people about a pet that both people know. Help children use the question-and-answer pattern of *Digby* as they write together.

Mrs. Murphy's Bears

by Katheryn Lilly; illustrated by Loreta Krupinski

Book 19
Fluent

Book Features
A narrative about a real person; sequence of steps followed to make something

SMALL-GROUP INSTRUCTION

Introduce   Tell children the title, author, and illustrator. Read aloud the dedication line on the title page. Explain that this book is based on a true story about Mrs. Murphy, a woman who was once a teacher. She retired, or stopped her teaching job, but has kept busy by making teddy bears that she gives to children in the hospital. Help children notice important information in the pictures, story, language, or words as you guide them through the book.

- (pp. 2–4) When Mrs. Murphy was *young*, she was a *teacher*. Now that Mrs. Murphy is old, she doesn't teach, but she makes *teddy bears.*

- (pp. 5–9) To make the bears, *First* Mrs. Murphy cuts the cloth. *Next* she sews it. Say *First* (*Next*). What letter will the word start with? The cloth is different colors. Some has *flowers* all over it.

- (pp. 10–11) Next, Mrs. Murphy takes the bears to her friends, who put the *stuffing* in. *Stuffing* is the soft material that pillows are filled with.

- (pp. 12–16) Mrs. Murphy drives to the *hospital* with the bears and gives them to children who are sick. She has her picture taken with the children and the bears. Then she goes back to her little house. *Tomorrow* she will make more bears. Say *tomorrow* and listen for three parts in it. Find it.

Read   Have children read the whole book softly or silently on their own. Coach them if necessary with appropriate prompts from page 41. Make notes about any processing difficulties they may have to help you select teaching points later.

Respond   Encourage children to tell or write about how they would feel or what they might say if they were sick and Mrs. Murphy brought them a teddy bear.

Revisit   Use your observation notes to make decisions about important teaching points that will be helpful. For example:

- rereading to help figure out new words

- recognizing that some words tell sequence (*Now, First, Next, Then*)

- reading three-syllable words (*hospital, tomorrow*)

Optional Extensions   **Partner Writing** Have children brainstorm items that they could make for children in hospitals. Invite them to work with partners to write and illustrate the steps for making them.

Teaching Tip
When observing readers, make sure to note and praise individual successes and strengths. Notice especially when a child appears to be employing recently learned reading skills and strategies to correct miscues.

Home Connection
If possible, allow children to take *Mrs. Murphy's Bears* home to read aloud. Suggest that after they read, they can ask family members to tell about any teachers they remember when they were in school.

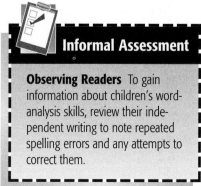

Informal Assessment
Observing Readers To gain information about children's word-analysis skills, review their independent writing to note repeated spelling errors and any attempts to correct them.

Book 20

Fluent

Teaching Tip

Help children make an "Animals and Their Homes" chart. List each animal from the book in one column and its home in the other. Then invite children to add other animals to the list. Encourage them to think of animals that have the same kinds of homes as the animals they read about. Talk about how sorting information can help you understand information as you read.

Home Connection

Children will enjoy sharing *Who Lives Here?* with their families. Encourage children to talk with family members about what makes a good home, for animals or people, and why.

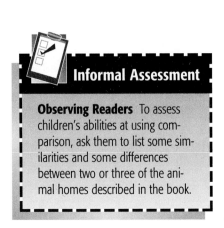

Informal Assessment

Observing Readers To assess children's abilities at using comparison, ask them to list some similarities and some differences between two or three of the animal homes described in the book.

Who Lives Here?

by Alec Rafter; pictures by Michael Adams

Book Features

Simple nonfiction text based on a familiar concept; strong picture support

SMALL-GROUP INSTRUCTION

Introduce Read the title and the author's and illustrator's names. Talk about what children's homes are like and why people live in homes. Then tell children that this book shows six different animals—a bear, a fox, frogs, a rabbit, prairie dogs, and turtles—and tells about their homes. On the last page, the book suggests finding out about the homes of four more animals. As you help children understand the book's framework, guide them to notice the information in its words, pictures, and structure. Invite conversation and introduce story words as necessary (shown in italics). Some suggestions follow.

- (p. 3) *People* live in homes, and animals have homes, too. Say *people* and find it. This book tells about some of the homes animals live in.
- (pp. 4–7) This bear lives in a cave. It sleeps and stays warm there all winter. And this fox has its home in the grass.
- (pp. 8–9) These frogs live in *ponds*. They like to sleep in the mud around the pond all winter.
- (pp. 10–13) Rabbits live *underground*. Say *underground*. What two words do you hear? Find *underground*. Look at page 12. These animals are called *prairie* dogs because they live in big areas of grassland called *prairies*. They dig *tunnels* underground to live in.
- (pp. 14–16) Here's a *family* of box turtles in their nest. And on the last page, there are four more animals. What are they? You will enjoy finding out where these animals live.

Read Intervene as necessary while children read the book silently. Choose appropriate prompts from page 41, making notes about children's processing of the text that will help you select important teaching points later in the lesson.

Respond Invite children to talk about which animal they think had the best or the worst home. Suggest they write a few lines in their journals explaining their choices.

Revisit Use your notes to address any difficulties children had and to choose helpful teaching points. For example:

- using comparison to understand and evaluate information
- integrating several sources of information to figure out new words
- self-correcting miscues by noticing when something doesn't make sense, sound right, or look right

Optional Extensions **Writing** Invite children to choose an animal from the last page, find out about its home, and use the information to write a paragraph in their journals.

Rereading Have partners read the book aloud to each other. Then suggest that they each choose a favorite animal and tell the information they learned about it in their own words.

The Lost Sheep

by Sharon Fear; illustrated by René Mansfield

Book 21

Fluent

Book Features

A humorous parody
of the traditional nursery rhyme
"Little Bo Peep"

SMALL-GROUP INSTRUCTION

Introduce Read the cover aloud. Talk with children about the nursery rhyme "Little Bo Peep," and recite it as a group. Explain that this book tells about where Little Bo Peep's sheep went when they were "lost." Guide children through the book, helping them notice important information and inviting them to comment on the story and pictures.

- (pp. 2–3) Little Bo Peep has lost her sheep. She asks, "*Where* did those sheep go?" Say *Where*. What two letters does it start with? Find *Where*. She cries, "*Yoo hoo!*" Say *Yoo hoo*.

- (pp. 4–9) She sees the sheep getting on a bus and she chases them, crying, "Stop!" Then the sheep go on a train (in a *taxicab*). Little Bo Peep is still behind them. The sheep ride the *elevator* up, and she is behind them again. The sheep ride the *escalator* down. She's almost got them!

- (pp. 10–13) *Uh oh!* Say *Uh oh!* One sheep jumps on a *subway* train. That's a train that runs in a tunnel underground. The second sheep flies off in a *helicopter.* There's the third sheep, on a boat. How does Little Bo Peep feel? How can you tell?

- (pp. 14–15) Little Bo Peep thinks she'll never find her sheep. If she leaves them alone, what do you think they'll do? The three dots at the end of page 15 mean that that sentence continues on the next page.

- (p. 16) Now that the sheep are home, Little Bo Peep is happy again.

Read Have children read the book silently. If necessary, use prompts on page 43 to provide support. Make notes about any processing difficulties children have to help you select teaching points for after the reading.

Respond Invite children to share which scenes they thought were funniest. Have them reread their favorite scenes aloud and comment on the illustrations.

Revisit Use your notes to select teaching points that address children's needs. For example:

- checking to see if what's read makes sense and looks right
- using known word parts and other sources of information to read multi-syllabic words (*taxicab, elevator, helicopter*)
- understanding a character's feelings
- understanding the humor in this twist on a familiar story

Optional Extensions **Writing** Brainstorm with children some things the lost sheep could do in your own city or town. Have children choose ideas from the list and then write and illustrate sentences about the sheep.

Retelling Invite children to tell in their own words what the lost sheep did.

Classroom Management Tip

To ensure that your work with small groups is not interrupted, emphasize independent work in classroom centers. If children work with partners, model for them how to work quietly and speak softly.

Teaching Tip

English learners may be unfamiliar with the nursery rhyme "Little Bo Peep," on which this story is based. To help them better understand and appreciate the humor in the story, introduce them to the rhyme in advance, using different illustrated versions.

Home Connection

Send *The Lost Sheep* home with children to read again. They might enjoy reading this book to a younger sibling or reversing roles and reading it to a parent as a bedtime story.

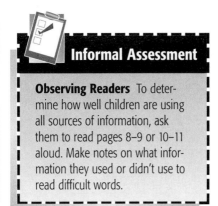

Informal Assessment

Observing Readers To determine how well children are using all sources of information, ask them to read pages 8–9 or 10–11 aloud. Make notes on what information they used or didn't use to read difficult words.

Book 22

Fluent

Anansi's Narrow Waist

retold by Len Cabral; illustrated by David Diaz

Book Features

African folktale
that relies on some patterned text
and picture support

Teaching Tip

Children might enjoy reading another Anansi story, such as *Why Spider Spins Tales, A Story from Africa*, retold by Janet Palazzo-Craig (Troll, 1996).

....

FYI

Children may be interested to know that even though Anansi is outwitted by his own plan in this story, in other tales he often plays tricks on animals and on people. In one story, Anansi tricks Tiger into swimming so he can eat Tiger's soup. In another, he tricks Elephant into thinking that one of the melons Elephant has grown can talk, making a fool of Elephant in front of the king.

Home Connection

If possible, send home *Anansi's Narrow Waist* for children to read to family members. When they return the book, talk about their families' reactions to it.

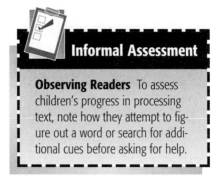

Informal Assessment

Observing Readers To assess children's progress in processing text, note how they attempt to figure out a word or search for additional cues before asking for help.

SMALL-GROUP INSTRUCTION

Introduce Read the cover and tell children that the spider is called Anansi. This book retells an African folktale that explains why spiders have eight legs and very narrow waists. Anansi wants to eat the food the people are cooking, but the food is not ready. So he asks the people to tie strings around his waist and to tug them when the food is done. Talk a little about what children think might happen when all the people tug on the strings at once. Then guide children through the book, pointing out important language patterns, words, and pictures.

- (pp. 2–3) Take a look at Anansi in the picture. He's a *spider*, but how is he different from spiders you have seen? That's right–he doesn't have any legs, and he has a big, round body. One day Anansi smelled *yams*, or sweet potatoes, cooking. He said, "*Mmm*–I love yams!" The people invited Anansi to eat soon, but the yams were not cooked yet.

- (pp. 4–5) Anansi didn't want to wait. So he made a plan. He asked the people to tie a string around his *waist* and to tug the string when the yams were done. What's a waist? Find the word *waist* on this page.

- (pp. 6–11) Anansi smelled other food cooking–rice and beans, and more. He used his plan again. Each time he smelled food he wanted, he had the people tie a string around his waist. As he moved *deeper* into the *jungle*, he had eight strings tied to his waist. Say the word *deeper*. What two letters are at the end? Find it on the page.

- (pp. 12–16) Anansi felt one tug. Then he felt another and another. All the people were pulling on the strings to tell him that their food was ready. Look at page 14 and see how the strings are tightening around Anansi's waist. What will happen to Anansi when those strings snap? On page 16, we see that Anansi has eight legs and a very *narrow*, or skinny, waist.

Read Have children read the story silently on their own. Support readers as necessary, using prompts such as those on page 43. Make notes about any processing difficulties children have to help you select teaching points later.

Respond Quickly make a story map with children, showing the setting, characters, problem, events, and solution. Then talk with children about Anansi's plan to get food. Do they think Anansi was smart to think of a plan like that?

Revisit Choose teaching points based on your notes. For example:
- recognizing sequence of events
- using familiar parts of words to figure out new words

....

Optional Extensions **Writing** Ask children to write a short paragraph on what they thought of the book, including whether they would recommend it to a friend and why.

Reading Children can read their book reviews aloud to the group.

Bears, Bears, Bears

by Nora Winter

Book 23

Fluent

Book Features
Nonfiction about a nature topic; photos

SMALL-GROUP INSTRUCTION

Introduce Read the cover, explaining to children that in this book they will read about and see photos of several different kinds of bears. Engage children in conversation about bears and what they would like to find out about them. As you guide children through the book, provide support for independent reading by pointing out information in its photos, language and words.

- (pp. 2–7) One kind of bear in this book is the *polar bear*. Polar bears live in cold places. Their fur and fat help them stay warm.
- (pp. 8–11) These brown bears wait for fish and catch them for dinner.
- (pp. 12–15) Bears who live in the woods can climb tall trees. They also eat berries, bugs, and *honey* that they find. Honey is the sweet, sticky stuff that bees often make in the holes of trees.
- (pp. 16–23) In winter, some bears dig dens or find caves to sleep in. Baby bears, or cubs, are born then. In the spring, bears leave their dens.
- (pp. 24–27) These pages tell again the important things that you have read about bears and warn you not to bother bears.
- (pp. 28–32) The words in dark print tell you that a new part of the book begins now. This part will list *Facts,* or true things about bears. Say *Facts* and point to it. The facts are listed for three different kinds of bears—**Black Bears, Brown Bears,** and **Polar Bears.** Many books about real animals, people, places, or events have pages like these.

Read Have children read the book silently. Intervene as necessary to prompt readers (see page 41) when they appear to need help processing the text. Make notes to help you select important teaching points after the reading.

Respond Invite discussion about the different kinds of bears in this book. Have children recall what they wanted to find out about bears before reading the book and ask whether they found out the information. Ask where they think they might look to find out more about these animals.

Revisit Based on the notes you took during reading, decide which teaching points will be most helpful. Some suggestions follow.

- stopping to check different sources of information when words or phrases don't sound right
- using pictures to build meaning for an unfamiliar topic
- understanding that books can give information as well as tell stories

Optional Extensions **Partner Writing** Partners can write and illustrate summaries of the information they read about one of the bears. Have children compile their pages into a classroom booklet.

Teaching Tip

Encourage children to reread *Bears, Bears, Bears* and to compare this nonfiction book with two other books in this Collection— *Mrs. Murphy's Bears*, a fictional story about some very different kinds of bears, and *Who Lives Here?*, another nonfiction book about wild animals.

Home Connection

If children take *Bears, Bears, Bears* home to read aloud, suggest that they ask family members where they have seen live bears or pictures of them. When they return to class, invite children to contribute to a list of places where bears have been seen.

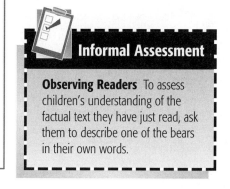

Informal Assessment

Observing Readers To assess children's understanding of the factual text they have just read, ask them to describe one of the bears in their own words.

Book 24

Fluent

Happy Birthday, Danny and the Dinosaur!
by Syd Hoff

Book Features

Humorous fantasy about a familiar experience

SMALL-GROUP INSTRUCTION

Introduce Read the title and the name of the author/illustrator. Ask children if they have read about Danny and the dinosaur before and what they know about the two characters. Talk with children about the scene on the cover, asking them to share experiences they have had at birthday parties and asking if they see something unusual about this party. Danny invites his friend the dinosaur to his party, and the dinosaur does some funny things. Help children notice important information in the language, pictures, story, or words as you preview the book with them.

- (pp. 5–11) Danny went to see his friend the dinosaur at the *museum*. Danny wanted the dinosaur to come to his birthday party. The dinosaur was *delighted*. Say *delighted*. Find it on the page. The dinosaur told Danny that he was a *hundred million years* and one day old that same day. Say the words *hundred million years* and find them on the page. Danny said the party would be for both of them.

- (pp. 12–19) The children helped Danny's father hang up *balloons*. Look at the picture on page 13. How did the dinosaur help? The dinosaur sang a song. Instead of clapping, though, everybody *covered* their ears. Why do you think they did that?

- (pp. 20–25) Look at the pictures to see more silly things the dinosaur did. When it was time to play pin the tail on the donkey, the dinosaur pinned the tail on himself. When Danny told the children not to put their feet on the *furniture*, where did the dinosaur put his feet?

- (pp. 26–32) When the birthday cake came out, Danny and the dinosaur made a wish. They wished that they would all be together again next year. That's when they decided it was the best birthday party ever.

Read As children read, support them with appropriate prompts from page 41. Make notes about any processing difficulties children have.

Respond Ask children what they think about Danny's inviting a dinosaur to his party. They can share unusual events from their own birthday parties.

Revisit Use your notes to select helpful teaching points. Some suggestions:
- using word parts to figure out new words
- linking meaning with personal experience
- recognizing sequence of events
- understanding that some events are real and others are imaginary

Optional Extensions **Writing** Ask children to write an invitation to the dinosaur, inviting him to their birthday party. They should include details about the party.

Teaching Tip

Children who enjoyed this book may want to read *Danny and the Dinosaur,* by the same author, to find out how the characters met.

FYI

Some children may not know that *pin the tail on the donkey* is a game sometimes played at parties. Explain that in the game players are blindfolded, one at a time, and then try to pin a tail to the end of a paper donkey.

 Home Connection

Invite children to take *Happy Birthday, Danny and the Dinosaur!* home to read to family members and friends. Suggest that they talk about special ways they celebrate their birthdays.

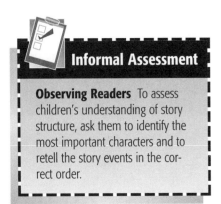

Informal Assessment

Observing Readers To assess children's understanding of story structure, ask them to identify the most important characters and to retell the story events in the correct order.

Henry and Mudge:
The First Book *(pages 5–22)*
by Cynthia Rylant; pictures by Suçie Stevenson

Book 25

Fluent

Book Features
Seven lively, reassuring stories about two lovable characters; comical, lighthearted illustrations

SMALL-GROUP INSTRUCTION

Introduce
(pages 5–22)

Read the cover to children, and show them Henry and Mudge. Talk with children briefly about what it's like to have a dog. Tell them that in the first four chapters of this book they will find out how Henry gets Mudge, how Mudge grows, and how they have fun together. In the last three chapters, they will find out how Mudge gets lost one day and how Henry finds him. Invite conversation about pages 5–22, helping children use the information in the book's language, pictures, and events. Suggestions follow for introducing the book's structure and some words in context (shown in italic).

- **Chapter 1** (pp. 5–8) Henry told his parents he wanted a brother. Then he said he wanted to live on a *different* street because their street had no children. But they said "Sorry" both times. Then Henry said he wanted a dog. His parents almost said "Sorry" again, until they looked at their house, their street, Henry's face, and each other. When they saw how lonely Henry was, they said, "Okay."

- **Chapter 2** (pp. 9–13) Henry *searched* for a dog. "Not just any dog," he said. He found Mudge, a puppy with floppy ears and straight fur, not curly. When Mudge stopped growing, he *weighed* one hundred eighty pounds and stood three feet tall! Henry was glad.

- **Chapter 3** (pp. 14–17) Henry used to walk to school alone, and he would worry about scary things, such as *tornadoes* and ghosts. But now he walked with Mudge, and he thought about fun things. Sometimes he even walked *backward*, because he wasn't worried anymore.

- **Chapter 4** (pp. 18–22) Mudge was happy, too. He loved many things about Henry's room. He especially loved Henry's bed because in Henry's bed was Henry. Mudge loved to smell Henry's *lemon hair* and *chocolate fingers*. Would you like those smells? Now you can read these four chapters to find out about Henry and Mudge.

Read
(pages 5–22)

Have children read the book silently. Intervene as necessary, using appropriate prompts from page 41. Write down any processing difficulties children have, and use your notes to help choose teaching points later.

Respond
(pages 5–22)

Engage children in a brief discussion of why Henry and Mudge like being together so much. Invite children to support their ideas by finding examples in the book and reading them aloud.

Revisit
(pages 5–22)

Use your notes to choose helpful teaching points. For example:
- using story details to make inferences about characters and events
- using language structure and patterns to self-correct errors or miscues
- self-monitoring to correct miscues when something doesn't make sense

Classroom Management Tip

Keep pace with children's current reading interests by changing the focus of your writing center from time to time. For example, you might display books, magazines, brochures, or advertisements about different kinds of dogs, pet care, or other related topics if children show an interest in knowing more about Mudge or other dogs.

For the remaining pages of Henry and Mudge: The First Book, *see the lesson plan on the next page.*

Book 25

Fluent

Teaching Tip

Encourage children who enjoyed this book to read more about Henry and Mudge, including the book *Henry and Mudge Get the Cold Shivers*, Book 26 in this Collection.

Home Connection

Invite children to take this book home to read to their families. Suggest that they talk about their own pets or other pets they know about and why people like to have pets.

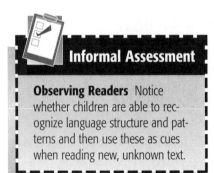

Informal Assessment

Observing Readers Notice whether children are able to recognize language structure and patterns and then use these as cues when reading new, unknown text.

Henry and Mudge:
The First Book *(pages 23–40)*
by Cynthia Rylant; pictures by Suçie Stevenson

SMALL-GROUP INSTRUCTION

Introduce
(pages 23–40)

Review the first four chapters with children, inviting conversation about what has happened so far. Then remind children that they are going to read about how Mudge gets lost and Henry has to find him. Guide children through these three chapters, helping them notice important information in the language, events, and pictures. Suggestions follow for preparing children to read and for introducing some story words (shown in italic).

- **Chapter 5** (pp. 23–27) One day Mudge went for a walk without Henry. He crossed a *stream* into some pine trees and got lost. Mudge couldn't smell or see anything he knew. He *whined* and lay down, sad and lonely. Say *whined*. It begins with *wh*. Get a good look at it. Mudge was alone.

- **Chapter 6** (pp. 28–34) When Henry got home, Mudge wasn't there. Henry thought Mudge would be with him always. When Mudge did go away, Henry's heart hurt because he was so sad, and he cried. Do you know how Henry felt? But then Henry decided that Mudge wouldn't leave him. So he went looking. When he got to the stream and the pine trees and called one last time, Mudge woke up and came running.

- **Chapter 7** (pp. 35–40) Henry and Mudge are together again. Sometimes, though, they dream about the time when Mudge was lost and each of them was alone. But when they wake up, they both feel happy that the other one is there. And Henry knows that he will never lose Mudge again.

Read
(pages 23–40)

Have children read the book silently. Choose appropriate prompts from page 41 to help children as necessary. Note any processing difficulties they have to help you select teaching points later.

Respond
(pages 23–40)

Invite children to talk about how Henry and Mudge felt when Mudge was lost and why they stay close together now. Encourage children to write down their thoughts in their journals.

Revisit
(pages 23–40)

Use your notes to choose helpful teaching points. For example:
- integrating various sources of information to figure out new words
- recognizing how word choices and language structure help readers understand what a character is feeling
- understanding how language, events, and illustrations work together to create memorable characters

Optional Extensions

Independent Writing Invite children to choose their favorite chapter from this book and to write a paragraph telling why they liked it the best.

Art Have children create "Lost" posters describing Mudge and telling why Henry wants to find him. Before beginning, suggest that they look back at the story to choose details they want to include on the poster.

Henry and Mudge
Get the Cold Shivers *(pages 5–25)*
by Cynthia Rylant; pictures by Suçie Stevenson

Book Features

A single ongoing story divided into chapters; realistic fiction

SMALL-GROUP INSTRUCTION

Introduce
(pages 5–25)

Read the cover, talking with children about times they have been sick and asking them to show the meaning of *cold shivers*. Explain that Henry is a boy whose pet is a very big dog named Mudge. Tell children that Henry and Mudge are characters in several other books by the author, Cynthia Rylant. This book is about what happens when first Henry, and then Mudge, gets sick. When Henry and his mother take Mudge to the doctor, Mudge shivers and he sheds because he's sick and also because he's afraid of the doctor. Read the table of contents. Then guide children through pages 5–25, helping them focus on important information in the language, story, pictures, and words.

- **The Sick Day** (pp. 5–17) Henry was sick. He had a *sore throat*, a *fever*, and a *bad cough*, so he stayed home from school. Say *sore throat (fever, bad cough)* and take a good look at the word(s). Mudge loved Henry's sick days. When Henry was sick, his mother (father) brought him *orange* (*grape*) *Popsicles, comic books,* and *crackers.* Mudge always got the crackers. Say the word *crackers* and find it. No one ever thought Mudge would get sick, until one day he caught a lot of germs—germs can make you sick. Henry and his mother were worried that something was wrong. What do you think was wrong? Yes, Mudge was sick.

- **The Vet** (pp. 18–25, first half) Henry and his mother decided to take Mudge to the *vet.* A vet is a doctor for animals. At first Mudge wouldn't get into the car to go to the doctor. He *yawned* and *drooled* on Henry's hand. Say the word *drooled*. What does it mean? Find it. When Henry said "Bath time," Mudge hopped in the car. But he didn't want to see the vet. She made him *nervous. Nervous* means afraid or worried. Say *nervous* and take a look at it. In the vet's waiting room, Mudge started to *shiver* and *shed*. Have you seen a dog or cat shed? What happened?

Read
(pages 5–25)

Have children read the pages silently. Intervene to support readers as necessary. (See page 41 in this manual.) Make notes about any processing difficulties children have, using them to help you choose teaching points later.

Respond
(pages 5–25)

Ask children to think about something Mudge might tell Henry or the vet if he could talk. What might he tell Henry when Henry is sick? What might he tell the vet about how he feels? Invite them to write their ideas and share them with the group.

Revisit
(pages 5–25)

Use your notes to choose helpful teaching points. For example:

- recalling personal experiences to help interpret a story's events and its characters' feelings

- recognizing that for emphasis, words may be set in different kinds of type

Teaching Tip

You may want to guide children through the first half of this book in one or two sessions, selecting appropriate parts of the following lesson plan for each session. The lesson plan on the next page covers the second half of this book and may also be presented in one or two sessions.

For books that will be read in more than one session, children can customize strips of paper to make bookmarks to mark the place they stopped.

For the remaining pages of Henry and Mudge Get the Cold Shivers, *see the lesson plan on the next page.*

Book 26
Fluent

Teaching Tip

For children who like the Henry and Mudge books, you may want to provide other Cynthia Rylant books about these two characters for self-selected reading. *Henry and Mudge: The First Book* is another Little Reader in this Collection.

 Home Connection

If children can take *Henry and Mudge Get the Cold Shivers* home to read aloud to family members, suggest that they read the first chapter aloud and then tell the rest of the story in their own words. When they return the book to class, ask them how their families liked it.

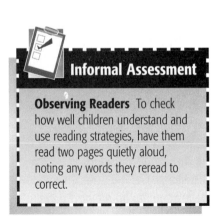

Informal Assessment

Observing Readers To check how well children understand and use reading strategies, have them read two pages quietly aloud, noting any words they reread to correct.

Henry and Mudge
Get the Cold Shivers *(pages 26–48)*

by Cynthia Rylant; pictures by Suçie Stevenson

SMALL-GROUP INSTRUCTION

Introduce
(pages 26–48)

Encourage discussion about where Henry, his mother, and Mudge were and what Mudge was doing at the point when children stopped reading. Explain that in the second half of the book, the vet checks Mudge. She tells Henry what's wrong with Mudge, and how to take care of him—but not to kiss Mudge until he's better. Invite children to predict what Henry does when Mudge's sick days are over. Continue to guide children, helping them notice important information on pages 26–48.

- **The Vet** (pp. 26–35, second half) In the vet's office, Mudge still shivered and shed. When it was Mudge's turn to see the vet, Henry's mother had to pull him into the room. The vet talked to Mudge and tried to make Henry laugh. But he was too *worried* and *scared.* The thought balloon beside Henry's head shows what he was thinking as he waited. He *wondered* if Mudge knew how to say "*ah.*" Say *wondered* and look at it. "*Ah*" is what doctors ask you to say so they can see into your throat. Say "ah," just like you do at the doctor's.

- **A Big Kiss** (pp. 36–48) The vet told Henry that Mudge had a cold—a fever, a red throat, and he was tired—just like Henry had when he was sick. Then the vet said to let Mudge rest and to give him his *medicine.* Say *medicine.* Clap the parts you hear and look at the word. Henry *frowned* when the vet said not to kiss Mudge "until he's better." Show what Henry did when he frowned. So Henry fixed a place for Mudge to rest and brought him ice cubes, a rubber *hamburger,* and crackers. Henry got the crackers. That evening, Henry brought more things and he got the crackers again. But who do you think ate all the crackers the next day?

Read
(pages 26–48)

Have children read the pages silently. Help readers as necessary to process the text. (See page 41 in this manual.) Make notes on any difficulties they may have to help you select important teaching points after the reading.

Respond
(pages 26–48)

Children can compare this book to another they have read about children and their pets. Ask them to tell which of the books they liked best and why.

Revisit
(pages 26–48)

Use the notes you took during reading to choose teaching points, such as the following, that will be the most helpful.

- using both pictures and text to determine how characters feel
- reading words whose spelling changes before *-ed* or *-ing* endings (*nodded, hopped, shedding, rubbed*)

Optional Extensions

Cooperative Writing Children can work in small groups to brainstorm and write another chapter that tells what Henry and Mudge did after they both got well.

Dogs at Work

by Elizabeth West

Book Features

Informational text with photographs; some concepts that may be new to children

SMALL-GROUP INSTRUCTION

Introduce Read the cover, and talk with children about the photo. Point out that it shows one kind of work that dogs can do—they can pull a sled. Explain that in this book they will learn about other work that dogs do, such as helping to find lost people, helping blind people get around, and even acting in movies. As you guide children through the book, engage them in conversation to draw out what they know about the topic.

- (pp. 2–3) Most dogs, like this one, are pets. What are some things that pet dogs do? If you throw a ball, a dog will *fetch* it, or bring it back. The dog in the photo can *shake hands*. But some dogs work to help people. The rest of the book tells about dogs that work.

- (pp. 4–5) Some dogs work in large parks, helping the *park rangers* find people who are lost. The dogs *sniff,* or smell, a piece of the lost person's clothing and then use the smell to *track down*, or find, the person.

- (pp. 6–7) This dog works at *herding* sheep. Find *herding*. Do you see the small word *herd* in it? A dog *herds* sheep by keeping the sheep together.

- (pp. 8–11) Have you ever seen a *guide dog* helping a blind person on the street or in a store? A guide dog helps the person get around safely. You may have used a sled to have fun in the snow. In some places people use sleds to get around, or *travel*. Dogs pull the sleds. The dogs work together as a team to make the sled run smoothly.

- (pp. 12–13) Just as dogs use their sense of smell to help park rangers find lost people, they use smell to help police officers find *criminals*. Say *criminals*. Clap the parts. Find it and get a good look at it.

- (pp. 14–15) Have you seen dogs in movies or TV shows? The movie *crew,* the people working on the movie, tell the dog what to do. The dog might have to do the *scene* over several times to get it right.

Read Have children read the book silently. When necessary, choose appropriate prompts (see page 41). Make notes to help you select teaching points.

Respond Work with children to list the different jobs for dogs that they read about and to summarize what they learned about each job.

Revisit Use your notes to select helpful teaching points. For example:

- integrating various sources of information to figure out new words
- using personal experience to build understanding
- checking new words by rereading for sense

Optional Extensions **Shared Writing** Work with children to choose one of the jobs they listed in Respond and to write a Help Wanted ad for a dog to do that job.

Teaching Tip

If children have read *Bookstore Cat* in this Collection, suggest that they compare the "work" that Mulligan the cat did in that story with the kinds of work described in *Dogs at Work.* You might also suggest that they compare the working dogs in this book with pet dogs that they have read about in the Collection, such as in *Digby, Henry and Mudge: The First Book*, and *Henry and Mudge Get the Cold Shivers.*

Home Connection

Have children bring *Dogs at Work* home to share with their families. Suggest that they find out if family members have had experiences with working dogs, such as the ones in the book, or if they know of other examples. Allow children to share this information when they return to class.

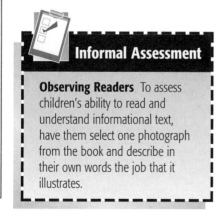

Informal Assessment

Observing Readers To assess children's ability to read and understand informational text, have them select one photograph from the book and describe in their own words the job that it illustrates.

Book 28

Fluent

Addie's Bad Day

by Joan Robins; illustrated by Sue Truesdell

Book Features

Humorous story about friendship, with fast-paced dialogue and nonsense words

---

Teaching Tip

Children who enjoyed this story might like to read Joan Robins's earlier book *Addie Meets Max* (Harper 1985), which tells about the start of the friendship between these two characters. Children might also enjoy comparing Addie's bad day to Alexander's in *Alexander and the Terrible, Horrible, No Good, Very Bad Day* by Judith Viorst (Macmillan 1972). Read the book aloud to them or make it available for independent reading.

 **Home Connection**

Have children take home *Addie's Bad Day* to read to family members. Suggest that they talk about bad days they have had and how they cheer themselves up on a bad day.

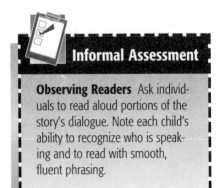

Informal Assessment

Observing Readers Ask individuals to read aloud portions of the story's dialogue. Note each child's ability to recognize who is speaking and to read with smooth, fluent phrasing.

SMALL-GROUP INSTRUCTION

Introduce Read the cover aloud. Talk with children about any really bad days they have had. Tell them that Addie, the girl in the picture, has a very bad day because she thinks she got a very bad haircut. That's why she's wearing the hat and why she doesn't want to go to her friend Max's birthday party. But Max convinces her that she *can* come to the party, wearing a costume so that no one will see her hair. Guide children through the book, engaging them in conversation about the pictures, story, and language.

- (pp. 4–7) Addie *peeked* around the tree, or "looked" around it. She didn't want anyone to see her.

- (pp. 8–12) Addie gave Max his birthday card and present, but she said she can't stay for the party because she can't take off her hat.

- (pp. 14–17) These pages tell something that happened earlier this morning. Addie got a haircut and all her hair was on the floor! (At least that's what she thinks.) That's why she can't take off her hat.

- (pp. 22–25) Look at Addie without her hat. Max told Addie that her hair is growing back, but of course it isn't. It wasn't really all cut off! Addie said she looks like an *ugly-wugly*, a made-up word. Find *ugly-wugly* and take a look at it. Max said then he must be a *pugly-mugly*. He was playing along, trying to make her feel better.

- (pp. 26–29) Max's present from Addie was a jungle suit. Addie has one just like it. Max said they can both wear their jungle suits to the party. Addie's problem is solved: no one will see her hair!

Read Have children read the book silently, and provide help as necessary. See page 41 for suggested prompts. Make notes about any processing difficulties children have to help you select teaching points for Revisit.

Respond Ask children what they think about Max. What kind of friend is he? What do they think of the way he solved Addie's problem?

Revisit Use your notes to select teaching points that address children's needs. For example:

- integrating various sources of information to figure out new words

- stopping to reread for meaning

- keeping track of who is speaking in the story

Optional Extensions **Writing** Ask children to write about a bad day they have had, a time when they felt like Addie. You can compile their writing into a Bad Day Book. Make the Bad Day Book available for independent reading.

The Grandma Mix-up *(pages 7–29)*

story and pictures by Emily Arnold McCully

Book 29

Fluent

Book Features

Realistic fiction;
a problem created by
two very different characters

SMALL-GROUP INSTRUCTION

Introduce
(pages 7–29)

Read the cover and the table of contents and discuss with children their understanding of the term *mix-up*. Explain that in this book the mix-up is when a girl's two grandmas both show up to baby-sit her at the same time. The two grandmas have very different ideas about how to do things and disagree on what the girl, Pip, should do. Grandma Nan has lots of rules to follow and Grandma Sal wants to relax and have fun. As you guide children through pages 7–29, help them notice important information in pictures, language structure, and words. It may be helpful to point out the words shown in italics below to some readers.

- **The Mix-up** (pp. 7–17) When Mom and Dad were going on a trip, Grandma Nan came to take care of Pip. Then Grandma Sal got there in a taxi. On page 13, you can see how surprised everyone was. The mix-up happened because Mom and Dad had each asked a different grandma to come to *baby-sit* at the same time. Grandma Sal said both grandmas could baby-sit, so Mom and Dad hugged Pip *good-bye*.
- **A Bad Start** (pp. 18–29) Grandma Nan (Sal) said, "Let's *get busy (relax)*." Grandma Nan wanted to *inspect*, or look closely at, Pip's room.   Grandma Nan was very *strict*. That means she had rules and made Pip follow them. Say *strict* and get a good look at it. When Grandma Sal said Pip was a "*super-duper* rider," what did she mean? Yes, Pip was a very good bike rider. Then Grandma Nan called *Hi-ho* to get their attention because it was *noon on the dot*—that means exactly twelve on the clock and time for lunch. Say *super-duper (Hi-ho)* and take a good look at the two parts of the word. The grandmas had different ideas about what Pip should eat for lunch. Pip said she wasn't hungry and Grandma Nan said, "A nap is in order." That means it was the right time for a nap. Grandma Sal did agree to a nap.

Read
(pages 7–29)

Have children read pages 7–29 on their own. Prompt them as necessary. (See page 41 of this manual.) Take notes on areas of difficulty you observe. You can use these notes after the reading to help you select important teaching points.

Respond
(pages 7–29)

Encourage discussion about the problem that Pip has with her two grandmas. Then have children write down their predictions about whether Pip's grandmas will ever agree on something, and what Pip might do to get them to agree.

Revisit
(pages 7–29)

Use your observation notes to make decisions about teaching points that will be the most helpful. For example:

- using personal experience, the story pictures, and what the characters say to interpret the feelings of the characters
- integrating the use of all sources of information to figure out new words

Classroom Management Tip

Continue to refresh the independent reading activities list by replacing some old ones with new activities, or by bringing back a few that were replaced earlier but that may still be appropriate. From time to time, before beginning a guided reading session, go over the activity choices with the whole class to make sure they understand what to do for each.

For the remaining pages of The Grandma Mix-up, *see the lesson plan on the next page.*

Book 29
Fluent

The Grandma Mix-up (pages 30–64)
story and pictures by Emily Arnold McCully

SMALL-GROUP INSTRUCTION

Teaching Tip

Children may wonder what happened to the letter Pip wrote and put in the desk drawer. Invite discussion about whether it got mailed or if it was forgotten and how the story might have changed if one of the grandmas had read it.

Home Connection

If children take *The Grandma Mix-up* home to read aloud, suggest that after they read, they ask older family members to share memories of their own grandmas and any old family photos they might have of them.

Informal Assessment

Observing Readers To gain information on children's word-analysis skills, point out misspelled words in any writing they have done with the group or individually. Ask them to say the word they intended aloud and to suggest other letter combinations that would sound and look right for that word.

Introduce
(pages 30–64)

Invite children to tell what they know about Pip's grandmas and why Pip seems to be unhappy. Remind children that each grandma thinks her way is best for Pip. But they finally agree to do things the way Pip wants to do them. Continue to focus on information from the pictures, story, language structure, and words as you guide children through the last chapters.

• **Worse and Worse** (pp. 30–41) Grandma Nan said, "Rise and shine!" She meant they should get up and act lively. Pip went upstairs to write a letter to Mom and Dad. She wrote that Grandma Nan was too hard and Grandma Sal was too easy. And she asked Mom and Dad to come home. Then Pip put the letter in the desk *drawer.* Grandma Nan made *stew for dinner,* but Grandma Sal wanted *pizza.* Pip wasn't happy and both grandmas were *grumpy.* When people are *grumpy,* they are mad or angry. Say the word *grumpy.* Take a look at it.

• **Doing Things Pip's Way** (pp. 42–64) Pip wanted to do things the way she, Mom, and Dad always did them. Grandma Nan said, "bed at 8 *o'clock.*" Say *o'clock* and take a good look at it. Pip said, "STOP, I do not want to do everything two ways. I want to do them *our way.*" Then Pip told them about "our way." One thing she said was, "I don't eat *vegetables* all mixed up with meat." Say the word *vegetables* and take a look at it. The grandmas agreed to try Pip's way. Pip explained what she did at bed-time—put on *pajamas, brush teeth,* and have a story read. Pip wanted to choose the story and have her grandmas "take turns reading it." The grandmas started to argue again. But then they laughed. After that they did almost everything Pip's way.

Read
(pages 30–64)

As children read the last two chapters, coach them as necessary. (See page 41 of this manual.) Make notes on any processing difficulties you observe. Your notes will help you decide on teaching points to emphasize later.

Respond
(pages 30–64)

Have children reread the predictions they made after the first two chapters. Invite them to discuss the clues or personal experiences they used to make their predictions and to identify those that matched what really happened.

Revisit
(pages 30–64)

Select important teaching points based on the observation notes you took earlier. Here are some possible points to use:

• using meaning and punctuation to determine phrasing and expression
• recognizing compound words (*grandchild, bedtime, bookshelf*)

Optional Extensions

Cooperative Writing Have children work together to make a chart that shows the ways in which Pip's two grandmas were different. Have them find and use words and phrases from the book in their charts.

Extending

The information on this page is meant to help you select appropriately leveled texts for children to develop effective reading behaviors. The descriptions are broad, and you should expect some overlap between Extending and other reading stages. To identify each child's approximate reading stage and provide the child with appropriate books, use your observation notes and the oral reading checks you have recorded for that child.

Most Extending readers

- read silently with good understanding
- read orally with phrasing and expression
- are able to read longer texts over several sessions or days without losing track of story and meaning
- rely less on print details such as beginning letters and word endings
- cross-check one source of information against another
- are able to recognize and discuss the similarities and differences among different books
- are able to write about concepts and information gained from their reading
- are usually able to identify and choose texts that are appropriate to their reading level

Children who exhibit many but not necessarily all of the above behaviors should be able to successfully process and yet be appropriately challenged by books in an Extending group.

Books suitable for Extending readers are longer and have more text per page but fewer pictures than the books in previous stages. Some are divided into chapters, each of which may be either a complete, self-contained story or one episode in a series of connected episodes that make up a single, longer story. Characters and plots are more fully developed but often in less direct ways. As a result, there are more opportunities for readers to make inferences and draw conclusions to create meaning. The nonfiction books use special vocabularies to explore topics in more detail, and they may use graphic organizers such as charts or diagrams to present or clarify information. In nonfiction, the biography is introduced, while folktales and legends are represented in the fiction. Books in this stage are

Frog and Toad All Year	*Thank You, Amelia Bedelia*
Frog and Toad Together	*Amelia Bedelia and the Surprise Shower*
Too Many Babas	*Bobo's Magic Wishes*
Zack's Alligator	*What's It Like to Be a Fish?*
Here Comes the Strikeout	*A Picture Book of Helen Keller*
Jamaica and Brianna	

Coaching to Problem-Solve

Since most readers in the **Extending** stage are comfortable and successful reading silently on their own after brief story introductions, they may require only minimal coaching. From time to time, remind these Extending readers to monitor, or self-check as they read. Reassure them that good readers sometimes ask for help after they have tried all the ways they know to solve a problem. To help you determine when to intervene, watch for slowed reading rate, or reading aloud and finger pointing by children who usually do not resort to these techniques. You'll also know that some support is needed when a reader's attention seems to be easily distracted from the text.

▶ To help readers refocus on the text when their attention wanders:
  Do you need help with something? Show me where you're having trouble.

▶ To remind readers to use what they know to help them read and understand the text:
  What do you know about _____ that would help you understand this?

▶ To encourage readers to use more than one source of information to solve problems:
  Do you know another word like that? Does it make sense here? What might help you decide if it fits?

▶ To remind readers to look for words and word parts they already know:
  That long word slowed you down. Did you remember to look for parts that can help you?

▶ To encourage readers to use a book's organization and format to help them:
  You seem puzzled by _____. Look back at the title (head) of this chapter (part) to help you understand what it's all about. How can the chart (diagram, map) help you? What does the chart (diagram, map) show about _____?

Note: *For a comprehensive discussion of coaching statements, or prompts, to guide the reading and for a more extensive list of leveled books for early readers, see* Guided Reading: Good First Teaching for All Children, *by Irene C. Fountas and Gay Su Pinnell, published by Heinemann.*

Book 30

Extending

Frog and Toad All Year *(pages 4–29)*
by Arnold Lobel

Book Features
Chapter book
about the adventures of
two animal friends

Classroom Management Tip

Children should be improving their ability to monitor their own reading. As they stop and reread to self-correct errors, ask what they noticed that made them stop. After they finish reading, praise and support their attempts to correct the errors.

SMALL-GROUP INSTRUCTION

Introduce
(pages 4–29)

Read the cover and identify the main characters, Frog and Toad. Talk with children about any other Frog and Toad stories they may have read. Explain that the two friends have adventures in each of the four seasons. Focus attention on the contents page and then introduce the first two stories, highlighting important language patterns, words, or pictures.

- **Down the Hill** (pp. 4–17) In this story, Frog wants Toad to see how wonderful the winter is. Frog got Toad out of bed and they *tramped*, or marched, through the snow. Say *tramped* and find it. Toad sat in front on the sled and Frog sat in back. "Here we go!" said Frog. When the sled hit a bump, Frog fell off. But Toad didn't know it. He kept on talking to Frog until a crow told him he was alone on the sled. Then the sled crashed with a *Bang! Thud! Plop!* Toad decided that bed was much better than winter so he went home.

- **The Corner** (pp. 18–29) In this story about spring, Frog tells Toad a story—about how he looked for spring when he was not much bigger than a *pollywog*, or young frog. Toad said the day was *spoiled*, or ruined, because it was raining. Say *spoiled* and find it. While they waited for the rain to stop, Frog told his story. One cold, gray day, Frog's father told him that spring was *just around the corner*. Say *corner* and find it. Frog's father meant that spring would come any day, but Frog went to look around <u>real</u> corners for spring. When he couldn't find it, he went back home. And there was spring—around the corner of his house. Frog's story was finished. The rain had stopped and spring had come again.

Read
(pages 4–29)

Have children read the book silently. Support readers as necessary, using prompts such as those on Teacher's Manual page 61. Make notes about any processing difficulties children have to help you select teaching points later.

Respond
(pages 4–29)

Talk with children about their experiences of winter and spring. Have they ever done anything like Frog and Toad did—gone for a ride on a sled or searched for signs of spring? Ask them to write about something they did in the winter or spring.

Revisit
(pages 4–29)

Choose teaching points based on your notes. For example:

- integrating various sources of information to figure out new words

- rereading to check for sense

- using familiar (or known) word parts to read new words

For the remaining pages of Frog and Toad All Year, *see the lesson plan on the next page.*

Frog and Toad All Year (pages 30–64)
by Arnold Lobel

SMALL-GROUP INSTRUCTION

Introduce
(pages 30–64)

Tell children that the last three stories are about Frog and Toad in summer, fall, and winter. Point out story structure, words, and language patterns as you guide children through the book.

- **Ice Cream** (pp. 30–41) This story tells how Toad turned into a "mo when he went to get ice-cream cones. Because it was a hot summer day, the ice cream melted and slipped and dripped and *splattered* on Toad. Say *splattered*. Find it on the page. Sticks and leaves stuck to Toad, and the cones stuck up from his head. Some animals warned Frog that an awful thing was coming. What do you think the thing was? Toad fell in the pond and the ice cream was washed away. So the two friends went and got two more ice-cream cones.

- **The Surprise** (pp. 42–53) In this story, Frog and Toad each try to surprise the other by raking the leaves on his friend's lawn. One October day, Frog went to Toad's house and Toad went to Frog's house. The two friends did not see each other. They each raked the other's lawn until all the leaves were in a pile. On their way home, the wind blew the leaves everywhere. Frog saw leaves all over his lawn. Toad saw leaves all over his lawn. Each thought about how surprised the other must be to find all the leaves raked into a pile on his lawn. Do you think Frog and Toad were surprised?

- **Christmas Eve** (pp. 54–64) The last story tells how Toad cooked a big dinner for Frog on Christmas Eve. Toad wasn't sure what time it was because his clock was broken. But he knew that Frog was late. Toad was *worried*. Say *worried*. Get a good look at the word. The pictures on pages 56, 57, and 58 show the *terrible* things Toad imagined happening to Frog. Just as Toad ran out of the house with a rope, a lantern, and a frying pan to save Frog, there was Frog. He was late because he had been wrapping Toad's present—a new clock.

Read
(pages 30–64)

Invite children to read the last three stories, intervening only as necessary. (See prompts on page 61 of this manual.) Make notes about any processing difficulties children have to help you select teaching points later.

Respond
(pages 30–64)

Talk with children about the friendship between Frog and Toad. Then invite them to write three ways that Frog and Toad are good friends to each other.

Revisit
(pages 30–64)

Select teaching points based on your notes and children's needs. For example:
- using multiple sources of information to build meaning
- recognizing that the setting can be important for understanding a story

Optional Extensions

Writing Children can write and illustrate a short episode about Frog and Toad based on one of the seasons. Encourage them to use dialogue in their stories.

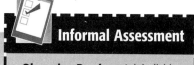

Home Connection

Encourage children to take home *Frog and Toad All Year* and read it to family members or friends. Suggest that they talk about their favorite story in the book and why they thought it was the best one.

Informal Assessment

Observing Readers Ask individual children to retell one of the stories. Notice whether they include the basic story elements such as character, setting, sequence of events, and ending in their retelling. If necessary, ask what they might do to help themselves remember what the important parts are.

Book 31

Extending

Frog and Toad Together (pages 4–41)

by Arnold Lobel

Book Features

Humorous animal fantasy;
each chapter is
a complete story

Teaching Tip

You may choose to guide readers through the first one, two, or three stories in this book, selecting appropriate parts of the following lesson plan for each session. The lesson plan on the next page may also be treated in separate sessions for the last two stories.

You may want to start a "Favorite Authors" shelf or a browsing box with other Arnold Lobel books, such as *Grasshopper on the Road* or *Mouse Tales*. For Frog and Toad fans, *Frog and Toad All Year* is in this Collection of Little Readers.

For the remaining stories in Frog and Toad Together, *see the lesson plan on the next page.*

SMALL-GROUP INSTRUCTION

Introduce
(pages 4–41)

Read the cover, explaining that this is one of several books by this author about two funny friends, Frog and Toad. Tell children that in every story about these two, they get into some kind of trouble. Read the table of contents with children and guide them through the text. Help them understand how each story works by pointing out information in its language, story, words, and pictures.

- **A List** (pp. 4–17) In this story, Toad writes a list of everything he plans to do one day. He made the list so he would *remember* what to do, and he crossed each thing off the list as he did it. Say *remember* and clap the parts. You can see Toad's list on page 6. When the list blew away, Toad couldn't run after it because that wasn't on his list of things to do. Frog ran after the list for him. Frog ran in low, wet places called *swamps*, and he *gasped,* or talked while breathing fast. Frog didn't catch the list and Toad said *Blah!* Then the two sat and did nothing until Toad remembered that *Go to Sleep* was the last thing on his lost list. So Frog and Toad went right to sleep.

- **The Garden** (pp. 18–29) Tell children that in this story Toad sees Frog's garden and wants to have one too. Frog gave him some flower seeds and Toad planted them. But the seeds didn't grow right away. Toad thought they were *afraid* to grow and must be the most *frightened* seeds in the whole world. *Afraid* and *frightened* mean the same thing. Toad did lots of things to get the seeds to grow and when they finally came up, Toad thought it was because he had worked hard to keep them from being afraid.

- **Cookies** (pp. 30–41) In this story, Toad makes a bowl of cookies to share with Frog. The cookies were so good that he and Frog ate *one after another*. They couldn't stop. They tied the rest in a box on a high shelf so they couldn't eat them. Finally, they gave the cookies to some birds. When there were no more cookies, Toad went home to bake a cake.

Read
(pages 4–41)

Ask children to read the stories silently. As they request help, use prompts such as those on page 61 of this manual. Make notes about processing difficulties you notice and use them after reading to choose teaching points.

Respond
(pages 4–41)

Invite children to tell which of the stories they liked best and why.

Revisit
(pages 4–41)

Use your notes to help you choose important teaching points. For example:

- recognizing known words and word parts in unknown words
- using sequence to build understanding

Frog and Toad Together *(pages 42–64)*
by Arnold Lobel

SMALL-GROUP INSTRUCTION

Introduce
(pages 42–64)

Review with children the troubles that Frog and Toad had in the first three stories, and read and discuss the titles of the last two stories with them. Continue to guide children through the last two stories, helping them notice important information in each story's words, pictures, and language. Pointing out words shown in italics below may be helpful to some readers.

- **Dragons and Giants** (pp. 42–51) In this story, Frog and Toad read in a book about brave people who fight dragons and giants and are never afraid. The two looked in a mirror and thought they looked brave, so they decided to climb a mountain to find out if they really were brave. On the mountain they got away from a snake with a wide *mouth* and from an *avalanche,* a lot of stones and dirt rolling down a mountain. Say *avalanche* and clap the parts you hear. Frog was *trembling* with fear. They hid from a *hawk* when they saw its *shadow*. And they kept saying they were not afraid. But they ran all the way back to Toad's house and hid for a long time. Each was glad to have a brave friend. They were feeling very brave together.

- **The Dream** (pp. 52–64) Explain that in the last story Toad dreams he is on a stage in a *costume*. A *strange voice* was *presenting*, or introducing, him as he did *wonderful* things. Say *wonderful* and clap the parts you hear. Frog couldn't do the things Toad could do, and he kept getting smaller and smaller. Then Toad looked out into the *theater* and he couldn't see or hear Frog at all. Then Toad woke up. He was surprised but glad to see that Frog was there, just like always.

Read
(pages 42–64)

As children read the last two stories, support them when necessary. (See prompts on page 61 in this manual.) Make notes about any difficulties you notice and use them to help you choose important teaching points later.

Respond
(pages 42–64)

Encourage children to compare Frog and Toad and to discuss which is the sillier and which is the smarter, based on the things each does and says.

Revisit
(pages 42–64)

Use your observation notes to help select important teaching points, such as:

- choosing and integrating several sources of information to check unfamiliar words

- recognizing word endings such as -*ing* and -*ly*

Optional Extensions

Partner Writing Have partners create a story map for one of the Frog and Toad stories in this book. Remind them to include the place it happened, the characters, and what happened in the beginning, middle, and end.

🏠 Home Connection

Allow children to take *Frog and Toad Together* home to read aloud. Suggest that they talk with family about things that Frog and Toad did together that are similar to things that family members have done with *their* friends.

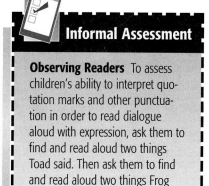

Informal Assessment

Observing Readers To assess children's ability to interpret quotation marks and other punctuation in order to read dialogue aloud with expression, ask them to find and read aloud two things Toad said. Then ask them to find and read aloud two things Frog said.

Book 32

Extending

Classroom Management Tip

Remember to keep guided reading groups flexible. Check children's progress frequently and re-form groups to accommodate children's changing needs and strengths.

Too Many Babas (pages 6–31)

story and pictures by Carolyn Croll

Book Features

A folktale-like story with a cumulative structure and a moral; set in Russia

SMALL-GROUP INSTRUCTION

Introduce
(pages 6–31)

Read aloud the cover and title page. Tell children that *baba* means "old woman" in Russia, where this story takes place. Baba Edis is the woman standing by the soup pot on the cover. One day when she is making soup, her friends, the three other babas, come to visit. Each baba adds something to the soup. Ask children if they have ever heard the saying "Too many cooks spoil the broth (or stew)." This story shows how that can happen. Guide children through pages 6–31, helping them to notice important information and to hear some of the language. Invite them to comment on the story and pictures in a conversation that builds interest and understanding of the story. Some suggestions follow.

- (pp. 7–11) It was a cold day. "This is a good day to make soup to *warm my bones*," said Baba Edis. Say *Edis*, and find the word on the page.

- (p. 13) This page tells what Baba Edis put in her soup. The soup filled the air with a fine *aroma*. Say *aroma*. What do you think it means?

- (pp. 14–17) Baba Basha was passing by. She got a *whiff* of the *delicious* smell and stopped in. She tasted the soup and thought it needed salt, so she dumped in a *fistful*. How much is a *fistful*? Show with your hand.

- (pp. 18–31) Next Baba Yetta (Baba Molka) stopped in. She added pepper (*garlic*) to the soup. Garlic is a plant something like an onion, with a very strong flavor. The picture on page 31 shows Baba Molka holding a garlic bulb. The little sections are called *cloves*.

Read
(pages 6–31)

Have children read silently to see how Baba Edis's friends "helped" her make soup. Intervene only if necessary. See page 61 in this manual for suggested prompts. Observe and take notes to help you select teaching opportunities after the reading.

Respond
(pages 6–31)

Invite children to discuss how Baba Edis might have felt about what her friends did. Have they ever had people try to "help" them in this way? How did that make them feel?

Revisit
(pages 6–31)

Based on your observation notes, select teaching points that will be helpful to children. For example:

- using more than one source of information to solve problems

- reading words with suffixes (*fistful, heavenly*)

- checking new words by rereading for sense

For the remaining pages of Too Many Babas, *see the lesson plan on the next page.*

Too Many Babas (pages 32–64)

story and pictures by Carolyn Croll

SMALL-GROUP INSTRUCTION

Introduce
(pages 32–64)

Review with children who the characters in the story are and what has happened so far. Then tell them that in this part of the story, the babas finally get to eat the soup, and it tastes *terrible*! They decide to start again and make some more soup, this time with a plan. Guide children through pages 32–64, helping them notice important information in the language and pictures and engaging them in conversation.

- (pp. 34–37) As they waited for the soup to be ready, Baba Basha, Baba Yetta, and Baba Molka added more salt, pepper, and garlic.

- (pp. 40–45) There are no words on these pages, but the pictures tell us what happens. Look at the faces of the four babas and the cat on pages 44–45. How do you think the soup tastes?

- (pp. 46–47) Here the words are in speech balloons, as in a comic. They tell us the soup is too *salty*, too *peppery*, terrible! *A little garlic goes a long way* means that garlic is very strong and you don't need much of it to add flavor. This soup has too much garlic!

- (pp. 49–51) The babas decide to start over and make more soup. This time they'll have a plan. When you finish the story, you will see how their plan turns out.

Read
(pages 32–64)

Have children read silently to see how the babas' plan turns out. Help as necessary. See page 61 in this manual for prompts. Make notes about any processing difficulties children have to help you select teaching points for Revisit.

Respond
(pages 32–64)

Ask children to compare the way the second pot of soup was made with the first. Can they think of other activities, besides making soup, in which it helps to have a plan? Record their ideas.

Revisit
(pages 32–64)

Use your notes to select teaching points that address children's needs. For example:

- recognizing elements of a cumulative story

- using predictions and rereading to check and confirm meaning

Optional Extensions

Shared Writing Review the babas' plan for making the second pot of soup. Work with children to write a plan for a familiar group activity. (See ideas from Respond.)

Home Connection

Encourage children to take *Too Many Babas* home to read to family members. When they return to class, have them tell how their families liked it. Did family members mention the old saying about "too many cooks"?

Informal Assessment

Observing Readers To assess children's fluency, ask them to read three or four pages aloud to you. Listen for expression, phrasing, attention to dialogue, and changes in rate of reading—all of which indicate children's flexibility in processing print.

Book 33

Extending

Zack's Alligator

by Shirley Mozelle; pictures by James Watts

Book Features

Engaging fantasy story with a mixture of storybook and everyday language; colorful illustrations

Teaching Tip

As children read, you might ask individuals to read a few pages quietly aloud to you. This will help you observe each child's processing abilities more closely and accurately.

Home Connection

Children will enjoy reading *Zack's Alligator* to family members. Suggest that children and parents talk about other fantasy stories they have read, such as *Happy Birthday, Danny and the Dinosaur!*, Book 24 in this Collection.

Informal Assessment

Observing Readers Assess children's understanding of realism and fantasy by having them list examples of realistic and fantasy story details from this book.

SMALL-GROUP INSTRUCTION

Introduce Read the cover and discuss the illustration. Explain that this is a fantasy story about Zack and Bridget, an alligator on a key chain who comes to life when Zack waters her, or gets her wet. When Zack takes Bridget outside, she gets thirsty, dries out, and shrinks back to key-chain size. But Zack promises to water her again tomorrow. As you invite conversation, help children understand what they see and hear in the book's language, pictures, and events. Here are some suggestions for building children's interest and for using context to look at some story words (shown in italics).

- (pp. 5–11) Zack gets a box from his uncle Jim in *Florida*. Say *Florida* and clap each part. Inside the box is an alligator key chain and a note telling Zack, "Water Bridget." Zack decides that Bridget must be the alligator, so he puts her in the sink to water her. Say *Bridget* and find it.

- (pp. 12–25) Bridget *stretched* and *sighed* in the tub. Zack fixes Bridget his Meat Loaf Special. Bridget says that back home in the *Glades,* she never eats anything like that. Bridget means the *Everglades,* a wet, swampy place in Florida where alligators live. Say *Glades* and find it.

- (pp. 26–41) Outside, Zack finds Bridget *wrestling* with something she thinks is a snake. Then Bridget attacks a mail truck. At the park, Bridget even sings! Look for Bridget's song on page 41, printed in italic type.

- (pp. 42–55) They meet Zack's friend, Turk, and Bridget sees a small dog, which she calls a *fuzzy-wuzzy*. But Bridget decides that she is thirsty, not hungry. Then Bridget starts to shrink because this place is too dry.

- (pp. 56–63) Bridget keeps shrinking, but Zack promises to water her every day. This makes her happy and she sings again. Back home, Zack puts Bridget in his pocket and smiles.

Read Have children read silently. Choose appropriate prompts (see page 61) and make notes to help you select teaching points after the reading.

Respond Invite children to tell which part of the story they thought was the funniest and to describe it in their journals.

Revisit Use your notes to select helpful teaching points. For example:

- talking about which story details are realistic and which ones are fantasy

- understanding what elements make this a fantasy story

- pausing to reread if something doesn't make sense

Optional Extensions **Writing** Children can write about Zack, telling why they think he smiles at the end and whether they would like to have him as a friend or not.

Rereading Children might enjoy rereading this story to younger children.

Here Comes the Strikeout *(pages 6–41)*

by Leonard Kessler

Book Features

Narrative about
a familiar childhood experience,
told mainly through dialogue

SMALL-GROUP INSTRUCTION

Introduce
(pages 6–41)

Display the book and read the cover. Talk about times when children have tried to do something that was difficult for them. Tell them that this story is about Bobby, a boy who is good at some things, like running and swimming, but not so good at hitting a baseball. Every time he gets up to bat, he swings three times and doesn't get a hit—he's a *strikeout*. His friend Willie agrees to help Bobby practice his hitting. Help children notice important information in the words, pictures, story, or language of the book.

- (pp. 6–13) It is spring and the boys and girls run to play baseball. Notice the word *BASEBALL* in all capital letters on page 8. This means that this word is read louder than the others. On page 10, we see Bobby. He can run the bases fast, he can *slide* into a base, and he can catch the ball. His problem is that he cannot hit the ball. He has had twenty strikeouts and he's in a *bad slump*, which means he hasn't hit the ball in a <u>long</u> time. Say *strikeout*. Do you hear shorter words you know in it? Can you find the word *strikeout*? Bobby's friend Willie tried to help him by lending Bobby his good-luck bat.

- (pp. 14–27) But when Bobby went up to bat, the other team yelled, "Boo, Bobby" and "Easy out." They didn't think Bobby would get a hit. And they were right—Bobby got strikeout number twenty-one. How do you think Bobby felt? Willie's lucky bat was not lucky for Bobby, so he returned it to Willie and walked home alone. During his bath, Bobby began to cry. His mother reminded him that he was a good swimmer and a good runner. He just needed to work until he was a good hitter.

- (pp. 28–41) Willie agreed to help Bobby but told him, "Only hard work will do it." On pages 30–31, Willie showed Bobby the steps to becoming a good hitter. Then they practiced. Willie told Bobby to just try to meet the ball with the bat. After a few tries, Bobby finally hit the ball. How do you think Bobby felt? Bobby continued to practice; he didn't give up even when there were bad days.

Read
(pages 6–41)

Have children read pages 6–41 silently on their own. Intervene when necessary, choosing appropriate prompts from page 61 in this manual. Make notes to help you select teaching points after reading.

Respond
(pages 6–41)

Talk about the main character, Bobby, with children. Have them write a brief description of what kind of person he is, based on what they have read so far.

Revisit
(pages 6–41)

Use your notes to choose important teaching points. Some suggestions:

- linking meaning with personal experience
- reading dialogue smoothly and with expression, as if talking
- figuring out unfamiliar words by using letters or word parts

For the remaining pages of Here Comes the Strikeout, *see the lesson plan on the next page.*

Book 34
Extending

Here Comes
the Strikeout *(pages 42–64)*
by Leonard Kessler

Teaching Tip

Tell children that phrases such as *Give him the fast ball* (p. 15), *keep your eyes on the ball* (p. 33), and *just meet the ball* (p. 55) have a meaning slightly different from the meaning of each word. Read pages 15, 33, and 55 and explain that *Give him the fast ball* means "pitch the ball fast"; *Keep your eyes on the ball* means "watch the ball closely"; and *just meet the ball* means "swing the bat so that it hits the ball."

 **Home Connection**

Invite children to take home *Here Comes the Strikeout* and read it with family members. Suggest that they discuss times when they had to practice and work hard to become good at something.

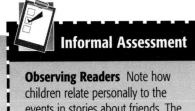 **Informal Assessment**

Observing Readers Note how children relate personally to the events in stories about friends. The ability to "step into a story" is one characteristic of a good reader.

SMALL-GROUP INSTRUCTION

Introduce
(pages 42–64)

Review with the group what has happened so far in the story, focusing on Bobby's problem. Explain that this part of the book describes the big game and how Bobby's hard work helps him get a hit. Walk children through pages 42–64, pointing out key language and words.

- (pp. 42–49) Before the big game, Willie had cheered Bobby on by saying, "You will get a hit in a game." When Bobby came to bat the first time, he hit a little *pop fly*—a short ball into the air—to the *shortstop*, the player between the second- and third- base players. At the *bottom*, or second half, of the fourth inning, each team had three runs. Willie hit a *long drive*, or hard-hit ball, to center field—it was a home run! A little dog ran off with the ball and it took a long time for the game to start again.

- (pp. 50–59) In the last inning, the score was still three to three, and there were two outs with a runner on third base. And who was up at bat? Bobby, of course. The other team thought he couldn't hit the ball very far, so they all moved in close to *home plate*, where the batter stands. Strike one. Strike two. Willie told Bobby, "You can do it!" The *pitch*—the ball thrown to the batter—came in fast. Then CRACK! POW! Bobby had gotten a base hit, and he was so surprised he forgot to run! The runner on third base ran across home plate. Bobby's team had won the game.

- (pp. 60–64) How do you think Bobby felt after his game-winning hit? Now Bobby strikes out sometimes, but he hits the ball most of the time. He says, "Only hard work will do it." It's something he learned from Willie.

Read
(pages 42–64)

Children can read pages 42–64 silently to see what happens to Bobby in the big game. As necessary, use appropriate prompts from page 61 in this manual. Any notes you take will help you select teaching points later.

Respond
(pages 42–64)

Invite children to discuss how Bobby changed from the beginning of the story to the end. Ask them how Willie helped Bobby and if they have friends who have helped them learn how to do something that was difficult.

Revisit
(pages 42–64)

Select important teaching points based on your notes. Possibilities:

- using multiple sources of information while focusing on meaning
- using predictions and rereading to check and confirm meaning
- understanding that sports such as baseball have a unique vocabulary

Optional Extensions

Writing Children can write a short episode in which Bobby helps Willie learn how to do something, such as swim, ride a bicycle, or play a game.

Rereading Children can choose a favorite scene in the story and dramatize it.

Jamaica and Brianna

by Juanita Havill; illustrated by Anne Sibley O'Brien

Book Features

Realistic fiction about friendship and feelings

SMALL-GROUP INSTRUCTION

Introduce Read the cover, inviting children to notice details in the picture of Jamaica (on the left) and her friend Brianna. Tell them that the story is about two friends who say things that hurt each other's feelings but that they make up at the end. Ask children to tell about times they have had their feelings hurt by what a friend said. As you guide children through the text, help them figure out how the book works by pointing out important information in its pictures, language, and words.

- (pp. 5–6) Jamaica had to wear her brother Ossie's boots until her mother could get her new ones. How do you think she felt about that? Her father said they were *unisex* boots, for either boys or girls. Her mother *scrunched* Jamaica's toes into the *tight* boots. Say the word *scrunched* and get a look at it.

- (pp. 8–15) There was a tiny hole in one of Ossie's boots. When she saw Jamaica, Brianna shouted that Jamaica was wearing "boy boots." That made Jamaica mad so she *jerked* the boot off and the tiny hole ripped wider. What do you think *jerked* means? At the shoe store, Jamaica didn't want to get boots like Brianna's. She got cowboy boots that had *curly designs*. Say *curly designs* and get a good look at the words. You can see the curly designs on page 14.

- (pp. 19–22) Brianna saw Jamaica's new boots and said, "Cowboy boots aren't in." What did she mean? Jamaica told Brianna that she didn't get boots like hers because they were *ugly*. How did each girl feel then?

- (pp. 24–30) Back at school on Monday, Brianna mumbled that her boots were "my sister's ugly old boots." Did Jamaica understand then how Brianna felt? Why? Then the two decided that when Brianna got new boots they could wear their new boots together. Are they still good friends?

Read Have children read the whole book silently, intervening only as necessary. (See prompts on page 61.) Make notes on any processing difficulties children may have to help you choose teaching points later.

Respond Have children tell what each girl said about her friend's boots and then write what they might have said to their friend if they had been Jamaica or Brianna.

Revisit Use the notes you took during reading to help you select important teaching points now. Some suggestions:

- using personal experience to help understand the feelings of characters
- understanding a chain of cause-effect events that develop a story

Optional Extensions **Independent Writing** Children can write about an experience they have shared with a friend and compile the pages into a class book.

Teaching Tip

Other books about Jamaica that you may want to add to a classroom browsing basket or box are *Jamaica's Find* and *Jamaica Tag-Along.* The books about Jamaica have good examples of dialogue in them so they lend themselves well to rereading aloud for expression.

Home Connection

If children take *Jamaica and Brianna* home to read, suggest that they talk with family members about any misunderstandings they may have had with close friends and if they became friends again.

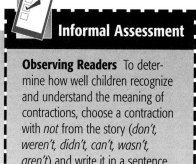

Informal Assessment

Observing Readers To determine how well children recognize and understand the meaning of contractions, choose a contraction with *not* from the story (*don't, weren't, didn't, can't, wasn't, aren't*) and write it in a sentence on the board. Ask children to read the sentence, point out the contraction, and say the two words that form it. Repeat for contractions from the story with *are* (*they're, you're*) and *will* (*I'll, she'll*).

Book 36

Extending

Teaching Tip

When children finish reading pages 6–37, work with them to list the words and phrases Amelia Bedelia mixes up in the story. They can refer to this list to refresh their memories when they finish reading the story in the next guided reading session.

For the remaining pages of **Thank You, Amelia Bedilia,** *see the lesson plan on the next page.*

Thank You, Amelia Bedelia *(pages 6–37)*

by Peggy Parish; pictures by Barbara Siebel Thomas

Book Features

Humorous wordplay, resulting in misunderstandings and silly situations

SMALL-GROUP INSTRUCTION

Introduce
(pages 6–37)

Read the title and the author's and illustrator's names. Ask children if they have read Amelia Bedelia stories and what they know about her. As necessary, tell them that Amelia Bedelia works for Mr. and Mrs. Rogers as a maid—she helps them by doing jobs around the house. Explain that in this story Great-Aunt Myra is coming for a visit, and Mrs. Rogers has many jobs for Amelia to do. But Amelia misunderstands the things Mrs. Rogers says, so she ends up doing the jobs in mixed-up ways. Some suggestions follow for helping children understand the story's framework—its words, pictures, story events, and language structure—and inviting conversation.

- (pp. 6–9) Mrs. Rogers was in a *dither,* which means she was nervous and worried. She wants everything to be exactly right so that Great-Aunt Myra will feel at home. Amelia tells Mrs. Rogers that she will fix everything.

- (pp. 10–13) Mrs. Rogers tells Amelia to *strip* the sheets off the bed. Amelia thinks she should tear the sheets into strips, so that's what she does.

- (pp. 14–19) Mrs. Rogers asks Amelia to *check* Mr. Rogers's clean shirts when the *laundryman* brings them to the door. Amelia makes sure all the shirts' parts are there. Then she draws a pattern of *checks*, like a checkerboard, on the shirts.

- (pp. 20–37) Mrs. Rogers asks Amelia to use spot remover to remove spots from her dress, to *scatter* some roses around the living room, and to *string* the beans. She also asks Amelia to make a jelly roll. To make a jelly roll, you spread jelly on thin, flat sponge cake and then roll the cake up with the jelly inside. Amelia does everything Mrs. Rogers asks her to, but in her own special way. Then she begins to mix up something of her own for Great-Aunt Myra.

Read
(pages 6–37)

Have children read silently. Intervene when necessary, choosing appropriate prompts from page 61 in this manual. As you observe readers, make notes to help you select teaching opportunities after the reading.

Respond
(pages 6–37)

Invite a brief discussion of what children think of Amelia Bedelia. How do they think Mr. and Mrs. Rogers will feel about what Amelia has done? Why?

Revisit
(pages 6–37)

Use your notes to select important teaching points. Possibilities include:

- understanding story language, wordplay, and humor

- integrating many sources of information to make sense of story events

- recognizing that many words can have several meanings and that people will sometimes interpret them differently

Thank You, Amelia Bedelia (pages 38–64)

by Peggy Parish; pictures by Barbara Siebel Thomas

Book 36
Extending

SMALL-GROUP INSTRUCTION

Introduce
(pages 38–64)

Briefly review with children what has happened in the story so far. Then tell them that this part of the story tells what happens when Great-Aunt Myra arrives and Mr. and Mrs. Rogers find out about Amelia's mix-ups. Some suggestions follow for guiding children through pages 38–64.

- (pp. 38–41) Mrs. Rogers asks Amelia to *separate* three eggs and *pare* the vegetables. Instead of separating the yolks from the whites, Amelia puts each egg in a different place. And instead of *paring*, or cutting up, the vegetables, she makes each vegetable a *pair* with another vegetable. Find *pare* on page 38 and *pair* on page 41.

- (pp. 42–56) "Stripped sheets!" Mrs. Rogers *exclaimed*. "What in *thunderation* happened to my shirts?" Mr Rogers roared. Say *thunderation* and find it. But now Great-Aunt Myra has arrived, so Mrs. Rogers goes into the kitchen. There she sees more of Amelia's mix-ups and puts her hand in a big blob of jelly, left over from Amelia's jelly roll! Mrs. Rogers exclaims, "Amelia Bedelia! How do you get things so mixed up?"

- (pp. 57–64) Then Amelia says, "Things mixed up! Oh, I *plumb forgot*," and hurries to the stove. When Amelia says she *plumb forgot*, she means she completely forgot about something. What has she forgotten? You can read the story to find out.

Read
(pages 38–64)

Have children read silently. As you observe, you might ask individuals to read quietly aloud to you. Choose prompts from page 61, and make notes to help you choose teaching opportunities after the reading.

Respond
(pages 38–64)

Encourage children to talk about why, after all Amelia's mix-ups, everything ends up all right. Children can discuss or write about times when they have mixed things up but had them turn out all right in the end.

Revisit
(pages 38–64)

Choose helpful teaching points, based on your notes. For example:

- recognizing cause-effect relationships among characters and events

- rereading to self-correct when something doesn't make sense

- discussing what makes a character interesting enough to read about in many different stories

Optional Extensions

Writing Encourage children to write a thank-you note from Great-Aunt Myra to Amelia Bedelia. Suggest that they reread pages 58–64 for ideas.

Interview Have partners discuss what Mrs. Rogers might say about Amelia Bedelia to someone who wanted to hire her. Then they can role-play an interview between Mrs. Rogers and the new employer.

Teaching Tip

Keep picture dictionaries or other student dictionaries in the classroom, perhaps in the writing center. Encourage children to look up some of the words Amelia mixes up. Suggest that they write sentences in their journals, using one or two of the words and their different meanings.

Teaching Tip

Children might enjoy reading another Amelia story, *Amelia Bedelia and the Surprise Shower*, which is Book 37 in this Collection.

Home Connection

Children will enjoy taking *Thank You, Amelia Bedelia* home to read to family members. Suggest that after they read, they talk with family members about any funny misunderstandings they have had with each other and how they worked them out.

Informal Assessment

To assess how well children understand the concept of words with multiple meanings, have them describe one or two examples from the story. Then encourage them to think of new examples of their own if they wish.

Book 37

Extending

Amelia Bedelia
and the Surprise Shower (pages 4–35)
by Peggy Parish; pictures by Barbara Siebel Thomas

Book Features

Wordplay
based on misunderstanding
of multiple-meaning words

SMALL-GROUP INSTRUCTION

Introduce
(pages 4–35)

Read the information on the cover. If children have read *Thank You, Amelia Bedelia* in this Collection or other Amelia Bedelia books, talk with them about what Amelia is like. If not, explain that she is a *maid,* a person who has a job doing household chores such as cooking and cleaning. She often gets into trouble by using the wrong meaning for a word that can mean more than one thing. For example, in this story, Mrs. Rogers is planning a special kind of surprise party, called a *shower,* for one of her friends. But Amelia thinks they are going to give the woman a *shower* with water! Guide children through pages 4–35, using the pictures to engage them in conversation.

- (pp. 4–9) Amelia's Cousin Alcolu is at the door. Say *Alcolu,* and find it on page 6. Mrs. Rogers and her friends are planning to give Miss Alma a *shower,* which is a kind of party with gifts. Amelia and Alcolu think this is strange because Miss Alma can give herself a shower. What kind of shower are they thinking of?

- (pp. 11–15) Mr. Rogers brings in some fish. He asks Amelia to *scale* them and *ice* them. He wants her to remove the scales (the hard material on the outside of a fish) and put the fish on ice. Mrs. Rogers had asked Alcolu to *prune* the hedge, or cut and trim it. Look at the picture on page 15. How do Amelia and Alcolu *prune* the hedge?

- (pp. 18–25) Look at how Amelia *scales* and *ices* the fish. What does she do? Next Mrs. Rogers asks Amelia to *run over* the tablecloth with an iron. She wants Amelia to rub the iron across the cloth lightly and quickly to smooth it out. Look at page 23. How does Amelia *run over* it?

- (pp. 30–31) Mrs. Rogers had asked Amelia to fix a bowl of *cut flowers*. The flowers were already *cut* from the ground. What do Amelia and Alcolu do with them?

- (pp. 32–35) Amelia and Alcolu decide to use the garden hose for Miss Alma's shower. What do you think they will do with it?

Read
(pages 4–35)

Have children read pages 4–35 silently. Take note of any difficulties you observe to help you select teaching points after the reading. If children need support, use prompts such as those on page 61 of this manual.

Respond
(pages 4–35)

Ask children which of Amelia's mistakes they found the funniest, and invite them to write predictions for what they think will happen at the shower.

Revisit
(pages 4–35)

Based on your observations, focus on a few teaching points. For example:
- understanding humor based on wordplay
- making predictions and rereading to check and confirm meaning
- using what they know to help them draw conclusions

For the remaining pages of Amelia Bedelia and the Surprise Shower, see the lesson plan on the next page.

Amelia Bedelia
and the Surprise Shower *(pages 36–64)*
by Peggy Parish; pictures by Barbara Siebel Thomas

SMALL-GROUP INSTRUCTION

Introduce
(pages 36–64)

Briefly review what children read on pages 4–35, and invite children to describe some of the preparations Amelia and Alcolu have made for the surprise shower. In this part of the story, children will see how the shower turns out. Guide children through pages 36–64, inviting comment and helping them use the illustrations to understand Amelia's mistakes.

- (pp. 36–41) The guests begin to arrive. Mrs. Rogers notices footprints on the tablecloth. She had told Amelia to *run over it with an iron,* meaning to rub the iron lightly over it. What did Amelia do? Next Amelia brings in the bowl of *cut flowers*. What has she done to them?

- (pp. 42–45) Miss Alma arrives late because she has a headache. Amelia and Alcolu are ready for the shower. Why are they wearing bathing suits?

- (pp. 46–49) Alcolu and Amelia give Miss Alma the gifts and a shower of water. Look at the picture on pages 48–49. What do the children do? What do the ladies do?

- (pp. 50–53) Miss Alma is very *angry*. Amelia thinks some tea will help her. When Amelia brings in the tea, Mrs. Ralph says that the chocolate looks good. What doesn't she know about that chocolate?

- (pp. 54–64) Mrs. Ralph bites into a chocolate-covered fish. How would you feel if you did that? She is angry! Mr. Rogers sees what Amelia did to his fish. How do you think he feels? But Miss Alma starts to laugh. She is the first one to see how funny all this is. Soon everybody is laughing. They decide that the shower was fun and that Amelia and Alcolu are wonderful.

Read
(pages 36–64)

Have children read pages 36–64 silently. Intervene as necessary, using prompts such as those on page 61 of this manual. Take notes to help you select teaching points after the reading.

Respond
(pages 36–64)

If children have read other Amelia Bedelia books, discuss what the books have in common, particularly their endings. Why do people always think Amelia is "wonderful" after she has caused so much trouble? Children can write their ideas in their journals and then share them with the group.

Revisit
(pages 36–64)

Use your notes to select helpful teaching points. For example:

- sustaining comprehension of a longer text over more than one session

- checking one source of information against another

- reading in meaningful units or phrases

Optional Extensions

Writing Work with children to make a list of some of the words Amelia mixed up (*shower, prune, scale, ice*). Have pairs of children work together to write sentences using the two meanings of each word.

Home Connection

Encourage children to take *Amelia Bedelia and the Surprise Shower* home to share with family members. If their families enjoy the story, they might look in the library for other Amelia Bedelia books to read together.

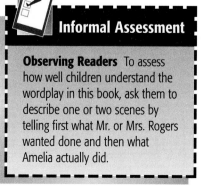

Informal Assessment

Observing Readers To assess how well children understand the wordplay in this book, ask them to describe one or two scenes by telling first what Mr. or Mrs. Rogers wanted done and then what Amelia actually did.

Book 38

Extending

Bobo's Magic Wishes

retold by Janet Palazzo-Craig; illustrated by Charles Reasoner

Book Features

A Puerto Rican folktale
with vivid, stylized illustrations

SMALL-GROUP INSTRUCTION

Teaching Tip

Discuss with children the map and information about Puerto Rico on page 32 of *Bobo's Magic Wishes*. You might want to show them the location of Puerto Rico on a large world map or globe.

Home Connection

Children can take *Bobo's Magic Wishes* home to read and enjoy with family members. Suggest that they ask family members if they know other story characters who are like Juan Bobo or other stories about magic wishes. Encourage children to share this information when they return to class.

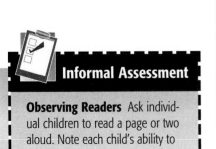

Informal Assessment

Observing Readers Ask individual children to read a page or two aloud. Note each child's ability to read the storybook language fluently and expressively.

Introduce Read and discuss the cover. Explain that the young man is Juan Bobo, a silly character who appears in many Puerto Rican folktales. In this story, the white horse gives Juan Bobo magic wishes. Juan gets into trouble, as he always does. But in the end he uses his magic wishes to make a sad princess laugh and wins a reward. Guide children through the book, pointing out important information and letting them hear some of the language.

- (pp. 4–5) There once was a young man named *Juan Bobo*. Say *Juan* (HWAHN). It begins with *J*. Because *Juan* is a Spanish name, the *J* stands for a different sound than it does in English. One night the king's wheat was *trampled*. Look at the picture. What do you think *trampled* means?
- (pp. 6–7) It was Juan's turn to *guard* the wheat. He ate a sticky dinner of bread and honey, then he fell asleep. Look at the picture. What do you think the ants will do?
- (pp. 8–11) The ants' dinner was Juan! "*Ow, ouch*," he cried. Find *ow, ouch*. Suddenly Juan saw a beautiful horse, and he caught it. The horse said, "If you let me go, I will give you seven hairs from my coat. Each hair will give you a wish."
- (pp. 12–15) Juan's brothers were going to the *castle*. There was a *reward* for anyone who could make the sad princess laugh. Juan wished that his ant bites would stop itching. Suddenly, he was covered in mud, the bites stopped itching, and the red hair from the horse was gone. From now on, each time Juan makes a wish, one hair will disappear.
- (pp. 16–31) Juan decided to go to the castle. Along the way he made wishes, and each time, one more hair was gone. When he got to the castle, only one hair was left. Juan made the sad princess laugh, and the king invited Juan to live with them at the castle. Juan still has the last hair. He doesn't need it, because he has everything he could wish for.

Read Have children read the book silently to find out what happened to Juan on the way to the castle and how he made the princess laugh. If necessary, support them with prompts from page 61. Observe and take notes.

Respond Juan's brothers did not think he was very smart. Engage children in a discussion about what Juan Bobo was like. Do they agree with his brothers?

Revisit Use your notes to select helpful teaching points. For example:
- using picture clues to make predictions and confirm meaning
- keeping track of sequence and cause-effect relationships

Optional Extensions **Writing** Invite children to imagine that they have the beautiful horse's seven magic hairs and to write about what they would wish for.

What's It Like to Be a Fish? *(pages 4–19)*
by Wendy Pfeffer; illustrated by Holly Keller

Book 39

Extending

Book Features
Nonfiction
presented through text
and diagrams

SMALL-GROUP INSTRUCTION

Introduce
(pages 4–19)

Read the title and the names of the author and illustrator aloud. Then read the title page, pointing out that the captions next to the fish tell their names. Ask children to share what they know about fish. In this book they will find out where fish live, how they swim and breathe, what they eat, and how they rest. Explain that while most of the information is in the words, some of the facts are provided in the pictures and diagrams, pictures that show how something works. Guide children through pages 4–19, helping them notice important information in the language, pictures, or words.

- (pp. 4–9) In this part of the book, the author tells where fish live. Fish live in lakes, ponds, *aquariums*, and, for very short periods of time, in plastic bags. A pet *goldfish* can live in a bowl.

- (pp. 10–15) How does a fish swim? It has a *sleek*, or smooth, body and fins. Look at the diagram on page 11. It shows a picture of a goldfish and tells what each of its fins are called. The skin of most fish is covered with *scales*. Say *scales* (*shingles, slick*). What letter do you expect the word to start with? Find it. Fish have scales covered with *slime*, a thick, slippery coating, to help them *glide* through the water. Fish swim by moving all their fins.

- (pp. 16–19) Here the author tells how fish breathe. People and fish *breathe* air. Look at the diagram on page 17. In the first picture, the arrows show how the air comes in the nose and goes into the *lungs* when we *inhale*. The body takes *oxygen* from the air. Say *oxygen*. In the second picture, the arrows show how the air leaves the lungs when we *exhale*, taking with it the *carbon dioxide* we don't need. The diagram on page 18 shows how a fish lets water in its mouth and takes the oxygen it needs from the water through its gills. Then the water and the carbon dioxide leave the fish's body through *gill openings*.

Read
(pages 4–19)

Have children read pages 4–19 silently on their own. Support children as necessary, using appropriate prompts. (See page 61 in this manual.) Make notes about any processing difficulties children may have to help you select important teaching points later.

Respond
(pages 4–19)

Ask children to find a fact that interested them the most and read the page aloud. Invite children to share any experiences they may have had with fish.

Revisit
(pages 4–19)

Use your notes to help you choose important teaching points. For example:
- integrating various sources of information to figure out new words
- finding out about similes (*scales overlap like shingles on a roof; They look as though they're flying through the water*)
- reading diagrams to support text and to acquire further information

Teaching Tip

Suggest that children read the captions naming the individual fish during a second look at the book to avoid disrupting the flow of text.

For the remaining pages of **What's It Like to Be a Fish?**, *see the lesson plan on the next page.*

Book 39

Extending

What's It Like to Be a Fish? *(pages 20–32)*

by Wendy Pfeffer; illustrated by Holly Keller

SMALL-GROUP INSTRUCTION

Introduce
(pages 20–32)

Review briefly with children what they have learned about fish from reading pages 4–19. Guide children through pages 20–32, highlighting language, words, or pictures that support meaning.

- (pp. 20–23) Do you know what fish eat? Goldfish eat fish flakes, which can be a *mixture* of *ground-up* flies, fish, *shrimp*, crab, oats, corn, carrots, and *vitamins*. Fish that live in the wild (those that are not pets) eat plants and animals so small you need a *microscope* to see them. *Usually*, big fish eat medium-sized fish, and medium-sized fish eat small fish. This is part of the food chain. Say *usually* and find it.

- (pp. 24–29) And what about the body temperature of fish? Fish are *cold-blooded*. Goldfish are most comfortable between 65–72 *degrees Fahrenheit. Fahrenheit* is a way to measure temperature. Say *temperature* and find it. You are *warm-blooded*. Your temperature is about 98.6 degrees Fahrenheit. Fish rest by moving slowly. Their eyes are always open because they have no *eyelids.* Fish live *naturally* underwater. Say *naturally*. What letter do you expect to see first? Find *naturally*.

- (pp. 30–32) The last three pages explain how to set up a goldfish bowl. First you put clean *gravel* in the *bottom* of the bowl and add a little water and *decorations*. Then you add water up to the *widest* part of the bowl. You float the plastic bag containing the goldfish in the bowl and after 15 minutes, let the fish out.

Read
(pages 20–32)

Have children read pages 20–32 silently. Use appropriate prompts from page 61 in this manual. Make notes about any processing difficulties children have to help you select important teaching points.

Respond
(pages 20–32)

Discuss what children discovered about fish from this book that they didn't know before. Create a word web of vocabulary related to fish. Children can make their own illustrated books of fish facts, using what they have learned.

Revisit
(pages 20–32)

Use your notes to help you choose important teaching points. For example:

- self-monitoring by stopping when something doesn't make sense and rereading to gain meaning
- recognizing that nonfiction often contains specialized vocabulary that is critical for understanding the topic (*scales, gills, oxygen, food chain*)
- using word parts to read unknown words (*protect, mixture, eyelids*)

Optional Extensions

Writing Have children imagine that they are fish. Ask them to write a journal entry telling about their daily activities, using the book for information.
Reading Children who enjoyed reading this book might want to reread other books of nonfiction, such as *Bears, Bears, Bears* and *Dogs at Work.*

Home Connection

Children may be eager to take *What's It Like to Be a Fish?* home to read aloud and to share what they've learned.

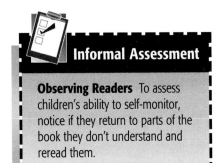

Informal Assessment

Observing Readers To assess children's ability to self-monitor, notice if they return to parts of the book they don't understand and reread them.

A Picture Book
of Helen Keller *(pages 3–19)*
by David A. Adler; illustrated by John & Alexandra Wallner

Book Features

A biography
with appeal and interest
for young readers

SMALL-GROUP INSTRUCTION

Introduce
(pages 3–19)

Read the title and the author's and illustrators' names. Explain that this book is a *biography*—a book that tells about a real person's life. This biography is about Helen Keller, who learned how to read, write, and speak, even though she was blind and deaf. Explain what *blind* and *deaf* mean if necessary. Ask children what they think it would feel like not to be able to see or hear anything. Then use the suggestions below to help them notice important information in the words, pictures, events, and language of pages 3–19.

- (pp. 3–7) Helen was born in Tuscumbia, Alabama. Say *Tuscumbia*, clap the parts, and find it on page 3. Do the same with *Alabama*. When Helen was about two years old, she had a *fever*, which means her body was too hot. Her mother put towels on Helen's *forehead* to cool her. Soon the *illness,* or sickness, was gone. But it left Helen blind and deaf. For Helen, the world became *forever* dark and quiet. Say *forever*. What two words do you hear in it? Find *forever* on page 6. It means "always."

- (pp. 8–13) Helen was often angry because there were many things she couldn't do or say. But she was also *mischievous*, which means she liked to tease and play tricks on people. Say *mischievous* and find it.

- (pp. 14–19) Alexander Graham Bell helped find a teacher for Helen. Her name was Anne Mansfield Sullivan. Helen called the day she met Anne her *"soul's birthday."* By this, Helen meant that meeting Anne changed her life—inside herself, Helen felt like a new person. Anne taught Helen proper manners—how to be polite, thoughtful, and considerate of others. Then she began teaching Helen a *finger alphabet* by spelling words in the palm of Helen's hand. One day Anne put Helen's hand under some running water and spelled the word *water* in Helen's other hand. Then Helen understood. She knew that everything has a name. From then on, Helen wanted to learn more and more.

Read
(pages 3–19)

Have children read pages 3–19 silently. Choose appropriate prompts from page 61 in this manual to help children through any processing difficulties. Make notes to use during the Revisit portion of the lesson.

Respond
(pages 3–19)

Ask children what they think of Helen. In what ways do children think Helen is like them? Invite children to write their ideas in their journals.

Revisit
(pages 3–19)

Select teaching opportunities based on your notes. Possibilities include:
- understanding that a biography is the story of a person's life
- using known word parts to read unfamiliar words
- connecting personal experiences with things they read about in the text

Teaching Tips

Page 16 Point out the unusual type treatment of *d-o-l-l* and *h-a-t*. Explain that the author uses hyphens between the letters to show that Anne spelled *each letter* of the word into the palm of Helen's hand. Ask children if they know how to make any letters or words using a finger alphabet or another sign language.

Page 32 Read through the "Important Dates" chart on page 32 with children at a time when it seems it will benefit them the most. For example, you might introduce the chart after children have read pages 3–19, explaining that they have read about some of the events shown and are going to read about the others when they finish the book.

FYI

Children may be interested in learning the finger alphabet that Anne taught Helen. *The Comprehensive Signed English Dictionary*, published by Gallaudet University Press, is one resource for this that may be available at your local library.

For the remaining pages of
A Picture Book of Helen Keller, *see the lesson plan on the next page.*

Book 40

Extending

Teaching Tip

During the introduction, you may want to begin a three-column chart with children showing 1) What They Know, 2) What They Want to Find Out, and 3) What They Learned. Help children list what they found out from pages 3–19 in the first column and any questions they have about what they will read next in the second column. After reading pages 20–32, return to the chart to fill in the third column.

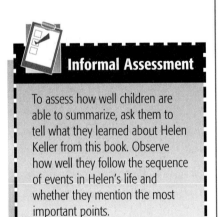

Home Connection

Encourage children to take this book home to read to their families. Suggest that they might enjoy taking a trip to the library with family members to find more books about Helen Keller or biographies of other people they would like to learn about.

Informal Assessment

To assess how well children are able to summarize, ask them to tell what they learned about Helen Keller from this book. Observe how well they follow the sequence of events in Helen's life and whether they mention the most important points.

A Picture Book
of Helen Keller *(pages 20–32)*

by David A. Adler; illustrated by John & Alexandra Wallner

SMALL-GROUP INSTRUCTION

Introduce
(pages 20–32)

Briefly review what children read about on pages 3–19. You might use the chart on page 32 to refresh their memories. Explain that the rest of the book tells about Helen learning to read, going to college, writing books, and helping other people. Read through the rest of the chart on page 32 with children, drawing their attention to proper names. Then guide them through pages 20–31. Some suggestions follow.

- (pp. 20–21) Anne Sullivan taught Helen *Braille*—a kind of writing made up of raised dots on paper that people can feel with their hands. Say *Braille* and find it. Helen also learned to speak, although not clearly.

- (pp. 22–25) At Radcliffe College, Helen was an *excellent* student and *graduated* with honors. During and after college, she wrote *articles*—pieces of writing that are shorter than books and sometimes published together, such as in a magazine—and books. She and Anne also *lectured*—talked to large groups of people, called *audiences*—about how Helen learned.

- (pp. 26–31) Helen visited *injured* soldiers during the Second World War. *Injured* means that the soldiers had been hurt in some way. She met many important people and received many awards before she died in 1968. But most important of all, she brought hope to *millions* of handicapped people.

Read
(pages 20–32)

Have children read pages 20–32 silently. Choose prompts from page 61 in this manual to help children through any processing difficulties they may have. Take notes to help you choose teaching opportunities later.

Respond
(pages 20–32)

Suggest that children find and read aloud a few sentences that tell what they found most interesting about Helen. What parts of her life would they like to learn more about? Have them briefly write their ideas in their journals.

Revisit
(pages 20–32)

Select helpful teaching opportunities based on your notes. Some possibilities:
- summarizing text already read before continuing on
- recognizing the sequence of events and using a chart, or outline, to keep track of it
- integrating sources of information to read and crosscheck new words
- discussing what makes a good biography

Optional Extensions

Writing Have children write a paragraph telling what they most admire about Helen Keller. Children can illustrate their paragraphs and then compile them into a book for later reading.

Oral Reading Check

Name _____ **Date** _____

Things I Can Do

I can ride a bike.

I can catch a ball.

I can dig a hole.

I can mail a letter.

I can read / a book.

I can paint / a picture.

I can do / lots of things.

Copyright © Houghton Mifflin Company. All rights reserved.

Words read correctly = _____ = _____ % (Score)
Words in book   36

Oral Reading Check

Name _____ **Date** _____

The Fox on the Box

The fox sat on the box.

The fox ate on the box.

The fox played on the box.

The fox jumped over the box.

The fox jumped on the box.

The box sat on the fox.

Copyright © Houghton Mifflin Company. All rights reserved.

Words read correctly = _____ = _____ % (Score)
Words in book   36

Oral Reading Check

At the Supermarket

I put the apples / into the / shopping cart.

I put the bread / into the / shopping cart.

I put the ice cream / into the / shopping cart.

I put the chicken / into the / shopping cart.

I put the milk / into the / shopping cart.

I put the bananas / into the / shopping cart.

Mom paid for / the food, / and I pushed the / shopping cart.

Copyright © Houghton Mifflin Company. All rights reserved.

Words read correctly = _____ = _____ % (Score)

Words in book   **60**

Oral Reading Check

I Want a Pet

I want a pet.

I do not want a very big pet.

I do not want a brown pet.

I do not want a black pet.

I do not want a white pet.

I want a green pet! Yes, I do.

I want two green pets!

Copyright © Houghton Mifflin Company. All rights reserved.

Words read correctly = _____ = _____ % (Score)

Words in book   46

Oral Reading Check

Name _____ **Date** _____

Mrs. Sato's Hens

On Sunday I went to see

Mrs. Sato's hens.

On Monday we counted

two white eggs.

On Tuesday we counted

three brown eggs.

On Wednesday we counted

four speckled eggs.

On Thursday we counted

five small eggs.

On Friday we counted

six big eggs.

On Saturday we didn't count

any eggs.

Copyright © Houghton Mifflin Company. All rights reserved.

Words read correctly = _____ = _____ % (Score)
Words in book   **51**

Oral Reading Check

The Good Bad Cat

The cat ran under the chair.

"Bad cat!"

The cat ran over the game.

"Bad cat!"

The cat jumped on the table.

"Bad cat!"

The cat saw a mouse.

So did everyone else.

The mouse ran under the chair,

over the game,

and across the table.

So did the cat.

The mouse ran out of the house.

The cat did not.

"Good cat!" / "Good cat!"

Copyright © Houghton Mifflin Company. All rights reserved.

Words read correctly = _____ = _____ % (Score)

Words in book   65

Oral Reading Check

A Mosquito Buzzed

Baby Bear was sleeping. / Snore, snore, snore. / A mosquito buzzed

near Baby's ear. / "Buzz, buzz, buzz." / Slap! went Baby Bear.

"Buzz," went the mosquito. / "Mama," called Baby Bear,

"Please get this mosquito! / I can't sleep!"

Mama Bear was sleeping. / Snore, snore, snore. / The mosquito buzzed

near Mama's ear. / "Buzz, buzz, buzz." / Slap! went Mama Bear.

"Buzz," went the mosquito. / "Papa," called Mama Bear,

"Please get this mosquito! / Baby Bear and I can't sleep!"

Papa Bear was sleeping. / Snore, snore, snore. / The mosquito buzzed

near Papa's ear. / "Buzz, buzz, buzz." / Slap! went Papa Bear.

"Buzz," went the mosquito. / "I'll get that mosquito," / Papa Bear said.

Crash! went the window. / Out went the mosquito!

"Now we can all sleep," / said Papa Bear.

All the bears were sleeping. / Snore, snore, snore.

Buzz Buzz Buzz Buzzzzzzzz

Copyright © Houghton Mifflin Company. All rights reserved.

Words read correctly = _____ = _____ % (Score)
Words in book   132

Oral Reading Check

The Secret Friend (pp. 2–13)

One day Squirrel found something / on his tree.

"A letter! A letter! And it's for me!" / Dear Squirrel,

I like you! / xxxooo / Your Secret Friend / (Can you guess who?)

"Fox," said Squirrel, / "Is this letter from you?" / "No," said Fox.

"I got one, too." / Dear Fox, / I like you! / xxxooo

Your Secret Friend / (Can you guess who?) / "Bear," said Fox,

"Are these letters from you?" / "No," said Bear. / "I got one, too."

Dear Bear, / I like you! / xxxooo / Your Secret Friend

(Can you guess who?) / "Moose," said Bear,

"Are these letters from you?" / "No," said Moose. / "I got one, too."

Dear Moose, / I like you! / xxxooo / Your Secret Friend

(Can you guess who?) / "Owl," said Moose,

"Are these letters from you?" / "No," said Owl. / "I got one, too."

Dear Owl, / I like you! / xxxooo / Your Secret Friend

(Can you guess who?) / The animals thought, / "Who can it be?"

"Surprise!" cried Snake. / "Your secret friend is me!"

Words read correctly =	_____	= _____	% (Score)
Words in sample	**156**		

(pp. 2–13)

Copyright © Houghton Mifflin Company. All rights reserved.

Oral Reading Check

Smile, Baby! *(pp. 2–13)*

Poppy wanted to take a picture / of the whole family.

"Come on, everybody," said Poppy. / "Smile!"

Mommy smiled. Rosa smiled. Carlos smiled.

Rags smiled, too. But not Baby. / "Come on, Baby," said Poppy.

"Peek-a-boo! Peek-a-boo!" said Poppy. / "Please smile, Baby."

Mommy smiled. / Rosa smiled. / Carlos smiled.

Rags smiled, too. / But not Baby.

"Maybe I can make her smile," / said Mommy.

"Booga, booga, booga!" said Mommy.

"Peek-a-boo! Peek-a-boo!" said Poppy. / "Please smile, Baby."

Rosa smiled. / Carlos smiled. / Rags smiled, too. / But not Baby.

"Maybe I can make her smile," / said Rosa.

"Watch the birdie!" said Rosa. / "Booga, booga, booga!" said Mommy.

"Peek-a-boo! Peek-a-boo!" said Poppy. / "Please smile, Baby."

Carlos smiled. / Rags smiled, too. / But not Baby.

Words read correctly = _____ = _____ % (Score)
Words in sample   127
(pp. 2–13)

Copyright © Houghton Mifflin Company. All rights reserved.

Oral Reading Check

The Three Billy Goats Gruff

Once upon a time / there were three Billy Goats.

The name of the goats was Gruff.

The goats were hungry. / They had to cross a bridge

to get grass to eat. / Little Billy Goat went first.

Trip-trap, trip-trap. / He met a troll. / "Hey," said the troll.

"I'm going to eat you up." / "Wait for my big brother,"

said Little Billy Goat. / "Eat him instead."

Middle Billy Goat went next. / TRIP-TRAP, TRIP-TRAP.

He met the troll. / "Hey," said the troll. / "I'm going to eat you up."

"Wait for my big brother," / said Middle Billy Goat. / "Eat him instead."

Big Billy Goat went last. / TRIP-TRAP, TRIP-TRAP.

Soon he met the troll. / "Hey," said the troll.

"I'm going to eat you up."

"OH, NO YOU'RE NOT," / said Big Billy Goat.

It was a good idea to cross the bridge. / The grass was yummy!

Copyright © Houghton Mifflin Company. All rights reserved.

Words read correctly = _____ = _____ % (Score)

Words in book   146

Oral Reading Check

Name _____ **Date** _____

Washing the Dog

To wash a dog, you will / need some soap, a large

tub, warm water, a bucket, / a rag, and a towel.

First fill the large tub with / warm water.

Next put your dog in the / tub. / Talk nicely to your pet.

Then pour warm water / over your dog.

When your dog is wet, rub / soap over its fur.

Rub the soap in with the / rag.

Then rinse your dog with / warm water.

Rinse off all the soap.

Finally, dry your dog with / the towel.

Copyright © Houghton Mifflin Company. All rights reserved.

Words read correctly = _____ = _____ % (Score)
Words in book   84

Oral Reading Check

Name _____ Date _____

The Crazy Quilt

Tanya found a quilt. / "What's this?" she asked her mother.

"It's a crazy quilt made from favorite / clothes," said Tanya's mother.

Tanya pointed to a spot of gray. / "What's this from?" she asked.

"That's from Uncle's favorite coat," / said her mother.

Tanya pointed to a spot of blue. / "What's this from?" she asked.

"That's from Grandpa's favorite shirt," / said her mother.

Tanya pointed to a spot of red. / "What's this from?" she asked.

"That's from Grandma's favorite / skirt," said her mother.

Tanya had an idea. / She found her brother's favorite shirt.

She found her sister's favorite skirt. / She found her father's favorite tie.

She found her mother's favorite scarf.

The next morning, / her father said, "Where's my tie?"

Her brother said, "Where's my shirt?"

Her mother said, "Where's my scarf?" / Her sister said, "Where's my skirt?"

And Tanya said, / "Good morning! Do you like my / new crazy quilt?"

Copyright © Houghton Mifflin Company. All rights reserved.

Words read correctly = _____ = _____ % (Score)

Words in book   148

Oral Reading Check

Name _____ **Date** _____

How to Make a Mud Pie

You can make a mud pie. / It's easy! / First, find some good dirt.

Fill some pans with water. / Dump the water on the dirt.

Mix the water and the dirt. / Now it is mud.

Mix the mud some more. / Use your fingers and your toes.

Put in some rocks / to make it crunchy.

Put in some fat, / wiggly worms.

Take out your shoes / and socks.

Take out your little brother.

Make the mud good and gooey. / Now it is ready.

Pat it. Make a flat pie. / Let your little brother help.

Put it in a pan. / Bake it in the sun.

When it is done, / give some to your dad.

Give some to your mom. / Give some to your dog.

Yum, yum, yum! / Everybody loves mud pie!

Copyright © Houghton Mifflin Company. All rights reserved.

Words read correctly = _____ = _____ % (Score)
Words in book   127

Oral Reading Check

Lift the Sky Up

Once upon a time, the sky was very low.

People bumped their heads on the sky.

Animals jumped into the sky to hide.

People got tired of bumping their heads.

People got tired of chasing animals / into the sky.

"We must lift the sky up," the people said.

"We must lift the sky up / when it falls asleep."

The people made long poles / to lift the sky up.

The next day when the sky was falling

asleep, three boys chased four deer / into the sky.

The people didn't see the deer. / The people didn't see the boys.

The people lifted the sky up, **up**, **UP**.

The sky was so high / that the boys and the deer / couldn't get down.

That night they turned / into twinkling stars.

We call these stars the Big Dipper.

Words read correctly = _____ = _____ % (Score)
Words in book   133

Copyright © Houghton Mifflin Company. All rights reserved.

Oral Reading Check

Name _____ **Date** _____

The Mystery of the Missing Red Mitten *(pp. 6–20)*

Oscar, I lost my other mitten. That makes five

mittens this winter. I'm in big trouble.

I'll search every place I played this morning.

First I went sledding with Ralph.

Here's Ralph's boot, but there's no mitten.

Oscar, if you were a bloodhound, you could track / down my mitten.

Look! Mouse tracks. / Do you think that the mouse and his family are

using my mitten for a sleeping bag?

I'll look around the castles we built with / Herman and Ruth.

Here's Ralph's other boot and Herman's sweater

and Ruth's sock. But no mitten. / Oscar! You found it!

Little bird, did you take my mitten? / Maybe a *hawk* did!

Do you think a hawk took my mitten to keep his / baby's head warm?

I wonder if I dropped my mitten while I was

making the snowman to surprise Miss Seltzer.

Copyright © Houghton Mifflin Company. All rights reserved.

Words read correctly = _____ = _____ % (Score)
Words in sample   **139**
(pp. 6–20)

Oral Reading Check

Name _____   Date _____

Nobody Listens to Andrew (pp. 3–13)

Andrew saw something upstairs. / He ran down very fast.

He said, / "Listen, Mother." / Mother said, / "Wait, Andrew.

I must pay Mrs. Cleaner. / She must catch the bus before / dark."

Andrew said, / "Listen, Daddy. / I saw something upstairs."

Daddy said, / "Wait, Andrew. / I must cut the grass before dark."

Andrew said, / "Listen, Ruthy. / I saw something upstairs.

It was in my bed." / Ruthy said, / "Wait, Andrew.

I must put on my roller skates. / I want to skate before dark."

Andrew said, / "Listen, Bobby. / I saw something upstairs.

It was in my bed on the sun / porch."

Bobby said, / "Don't bother me, Andrew.

I must find my bat and ball. / I want to play ball before dark."

Andrew said, / "Listen, Mr. Neighbor. / I saw something upstairs.

It was in my bed on the sun porch. / It was black." / Mr. Neighbor said,

"Never mind, Andrew. / I must take my dog for a walk / before dark."

Words read correctly = _____ = _____ % (Score)

Words in sample   **152**
(pp. 3–13)

Copyright © Houghton Mifflin Company. All rights reserved.

Oral Reading Check

Name _____ Date _____

Bookstore Cat (pp. 4–23)

This is Mulligan. / Mulligan is / a working cat. / He works in a bookstore.

His jobs / are . . . / doorman, / mouse-catcher, / watchcat,

and / baby-sitter. / Mulligan is / also great at / picking out

books . . . / . . . and entertaining / customers! / One day, the bookseller

made a new sign / for the window. / Mulligan was curious

about the new sign. / He kept / an eye on it / all morning.

Soon the bookstore / was very busy. / But Mulligan / didn't notice.

He had just spotted / a pigeon. / In the bookstore, / everyone was watching

a show. / In the bookstore window, / Mulligan was watching / the pigeon.

Just then a customer / came in. / Right behind her / came the pigeon.

No one noticed. / No one except / Mulligan, that is! / "NO BIRDS

IN THE STORE!" / meowed Mulligan. / But the pigeon / didn't leave.

"Okay," thought Mulligan. / "Time to get to work!" / Mulligan sprang

into action. / So did the pigeon. / The pigeon landed right

next to a funny-looking / green bird. / "Oh, no!" / Mulligan thought.

"Now there are TWO / birds in the bookstore!"

Words read correctly = _____ = _____ % (Score)

Words in sample   **165**
(pp. 4–23)

Copyright © Houghton Mifflin Company. All rights reserved.

Oral Reading Check

Digby (pp. 5–25)

Come on, Digby. / Let's play with my new ball. / Run, Digby!

Catch the ball! / Digby can't play catch / with you. / Why not?

Come on, Digby. / You can do it! / Digby is too old / to play catch with you.

How do you know? / Because I am older / and I know more.

Digby is too old to play. / See the way she walks? / How old is Digby?

Old for a dog. / Digby was here / before I was born.

Here is a picture of her / with me when I was little.

Did Digby play with you? / Yes, and Digby helped me / learn to walk.

Did Digby help me walk? / No, I helped you walk.

What else did you and Digby do? / We played catch. / Digby ran very fast.

Sometimes she hid the ball. / Could Digby do tricks? / Could she roll over?

Yes, and Digby could shake / and jump a stick. / Jump, Digby!

I told you / Digby can't jump now. / She is too old to jump.

What can Digby do now? / She can still shake and go for walks.

And she can still be our friend. / Digby can do other things / better now.

Words read correctly = _____ = _____ % (Score)

Words in sample   **189**
(pp. 5–25)

Copyright © Houghton Mifflin Company. All rights reserved.

Oral Reading Check

Name _____ **Date** _____

Mrs. Murphy's Bears (pp. 2–14)

Mrs. Murphy lives in a / little house near the woods.

When Mrs. Murphy was young, / she was a teacher.

All the children loved her.

Now Mrs. Murphy is old. / Now she makes teddy bears.

First she cuts the cloth. / She cuts red cloth and

blue cloth, and cloth with / flowers all over it.

Next Mrs. Murphy sews the cloth. / She sews the bear's arms and

legs and head. / She sews on two ears. / Mrs. Murphy finds two buttons.

She sews them on. She gives / the bear eyes. / Then she gives the bear

a black nose. / Next Mrs. Murphy takes the teddy / bears to her friends.

She and her friends put / stuffing in the teddy bears.

The bears get fat and round. / Now the teddy bears are done.

Mrs. Murphy puts them in her car.

She drives to the hospital. / Out come the teddy bears!

Mrs. Murphy gives the teddy bears / to children who are sick.

Words read correctly = _____ = _____ % (Score)

Words in sample 155

(pp. 2–14)

Copyright © Houghton Mifflin Company. All rights reserved.

Oral Reading Check

Name _____   Date _____

Who Lives Here? *(pp. 3–11)*

Who lives in these homes? People / live here. People sleep and stay

warm in their homes. / Animals have homes, too. But what

do their homes look like? Do they / sleep there? Do they stay warm

there? / This book tells about where / animals live.

Look at this bear in its home. This / bear's home is in a cave. The bear

will sleep in its cave to stay warm / during the winter.

Do you see the fox in the grass? / The fox sleeps here all day. Then it

goes out at night to look for food to / eat.

How would you like a home in the

mud? That's what these frogs like! They

like to live in ponds. The frogs sleep in / the mud all winter.

Rabbits live in holes under the ground.

They like to stay at home all day and go

out at night. What other animal lives

underground? Keep reading to find out.

Copyright © Houghton Mifflin Company. All rights reserved.

Words read correctly = _____ = _____ % (Score)

Words in sample   **154**
(pp. 3–11)

Oral Reading Check

The Lost Sheep *(pp. 2–11)*

Little Bo Peep has lost her sheep / and doesn't know where to find them.

Where did those sheep go? / "Yoo hoo! Sheep!" cries Little Bo Peep.

"Where are you?" / Look! There they go! / They're getting on a bus!

And there goes Little Bo Peep. / She is right behind them.

"Stop, sheep!" she cries. / "Come back here!" / Look! There they go!

They're riding on a train, / and Little Bo Peep is behind them.

Here they come! / They're in a taxicab,

and Little Bo Peep is still behind them.

The sheep ride the elevator up.

Up goes Little Bo Peep, right behind them. / She's getting closer!

The sheep ride the escalator down.

Down comes Little Bo Peep, right behind them.

She's almost got them now! / Uh oh! / What are those sheep up to?

The first sheep jumps on a subway train.

The second sheep flies off in a helicopter. / But where is the third sheep?

Words read correctly = _____ = _____ % (Score)
Words in sample   **153**
(pp. 2–11)

Copyright © Houghton Mifflin Company. All rights reserved.

Oral Reading Check

Name _____ Date _____

Anansi's Narrow Waist

One day Anansi the spider / smelled yams cooking.

"Mmm, I love yams!" he said. / "Come," the people shouted.

"We'll eat soon."

Anansi didn't want to wait. / "Tie a string around my waist," / he said.

"Tug the string when the yams are / done. Then I'll come back."

Anansi kept walking. / He smelled rice and beans cooking.

"Mmm, I love rice and beans!" he said.

"Come," the people shouted. / "We'll eat soon."

Anansi didn't want to wait. / "Tie a string around my waist," / he said.

"Tug the string when the rice and / beans are done. Then I'll come back."

Anansi kept moving deeper / into the jungle.

Soon he had eight strings tied / to his waist.

He felt a tug. "Oooh! Yams!" he said. / Another tug. "Oooh! Rice and beans!"

he said. / He felt another tug and then another. / The strings got

tighter and tighter. / Then they **snapped!**

Now you know why spiders have / eight legs and very narrow waists.

Words read correctly = _____ = _____ % (Score)
Words in book　　　　　157

Copyright © Houghton Mifflin Company. All rights reserved.

Oral Reading Check

Name _____ Date _____

Bears, Bears, Bears *(pp. 2–13)*

There are many kinds of bears. There

are brown bears, black bears, and polar

bears. This book tells about the food / bears eat and the places they live.

Some bears are black and other bears are

white. Some bears are small and other / bears are very big.

Polar bears live in cold places. Their / fur and fat help them stay warm.

Brown bears like to eat fish. / They wait for fish to swim by so

they can catch them and eat them / for dinner.

The bear sees a fish in the water. It

jumps and catches the fish in its mouth.

Sometimes the bear eats eight fish for / one meal.

Some bears live in the deep, dark woods.

They eat wild berries, bugs, and honey.

This black bear has sharp claws that help it

climb tall trees. There is tasty honey to eat / at the top of trees.

Words read correctly = _____ = _____ % (Score)

Words in sample   **148**

(pp. 2–13)

Copyright © Houghton Mifflin Company. All rights reserved.

Oral Reading Check

Name _____ Date _____

Happy Birthday, Danny and the Dinosaur! *(pp. 5–23)*

Danny was in a hurry. / He had to see his friend / the dinosaur.

"I'm six years old today," / said Danny. / "Will you come

to my birthday party?" / "I would be delighted," / said the dinosaur.

Danny rode the dinosaur / out of the museum. / On the way

they picked up Danny's friends. / "Today I'm a hundred million years

and one day old," said the dinosaur. / "Then it can be your party too!"

said Danny. / The children helped Danny's father / hang up balloons.

"See, I can help too," / said the dinosaur.

Danny's mother gave out party hats. / "How do I look?" / asked the dinosaur.

"We would like to sing a song," / said a girl and a boy. / They sang,

and everybody clapped their hands. / "I can sing too," said the dinosaur.

He sang, / and everybody covered their ears. / "Let's play pin the tail

on the donkey," said Danny. / The dinosaur pinned the tail / on himself!

The children sat down to rest. / "Please don't put your feet

on the furniture," said Danny. / The dinosaur put his feet / out the window.

Copyright © Houghton Mifflin Company. All rights reserved.

Words read correctly = _____ = _____ % (Score)

Words in sample   **176**

(pp. 5–23)

Oral Reading Check

Name _____   **Date** _____

Henry and Mudge: The First Book *(pp. 5–10)*

Henry / Henry had no brothers / and no sisters.

"I want a brother," / he told his parents. / "Sorry," they said.

Henry had no friends on his street. / "I want to live

on a different street," / he told his parents. / "Sorry," they said.

Henry had no pets / at home. / "I want to have a dog,"

he told his parents. / "Sorry," they *almost* said. / But first they looked

at their house / with no brothers and sisters. / Then they looked

at their street / with no children. / Then they looked / at Henry's face.

Then they looked at each other. / "Okay," they said.

"I want to hug you!" / Henry told his parents. / And he did.

Mudge / Henry searched for a dog. / "Not just any dog," said Henry.

"Not a short one," he said. / "Not a curly one," he said.

"And no pointed ears." / Then he found Mudge. / Mudge had floppy ears,

not pointed. / And Mudge had straight fur, / not curly.

But Mudge was short. / "Because he's a puppy," / Henry said. / "He'll grow."

Copyright © Houghton Mifflin Company. All rights reserved.

Words read correctly = _____ = _____ % (Score)

Words in sample   **166**

(pp. 5–10)

Oral Reading Check

Name _____ Date _____

Henry and Mudge Get the Cold Shivers *(pp. 5–16)*

The Sick Day / Henry's big dog Mudge / loved Henry's sick days.

When Henry had a sore throat / or a fever / or a bad cough,

he stayed home / from school in bed. / In the morning

Henry's mother brought him / orange Popsicles, / comic books,

and crackers. / Mudge got the crackers. / In the evening

Henry's father brought him / grape Popsicles, / comic books,

and crackers. / Mudge got the crackers again. / Mudge *loved* sick days.

But even though he loved / Henry's sick days, / no one ever thought

that *Mudge* would get sick. / No one ever thought

that Mudge could catch germs. / But he could, / and one day he caught

a lot of them. / When Henry woke up / and jumped out of bed,

Mudge didn't move. / He didn't get up. / He didn't lick Henry's face.

He didn't even shake Henry's hand, / and he always shook Henry's hand

in the morning. / He just looked at Henry / and wagged his tail a little.

Henry and Henry's mother / looked at Mudge and worried.

Copyright © Houghton Mifflin Company. All rights reserved.

Words read correctly = _____ = _____ % (Score)

Words in sample　　　　　**164**

(pp. 5–16)

Oral Reading Check

Name _____ **Date** _____

Dogs at Work *(pp. 3–7)*

Most dogs are pets. They can be good

friends. They'll run and play with you.

They'll fetch sticks or balls. Some dogs will

even learn how to do tricks. This girl has / taught her dog to shake hands.

But some dogs have work to do. Dogs

help people in many ways. This book tells / about the work that some dogs do.

These dogs have a good sense of smell.

They help park rangers find people who are

lost. The ranger lets the dog sniff a piece of

clothing from the lost person. Then the dog

can use the smell to track down the person.

This dog works at herding sheep. This

means the dog has been trained to keep the

group of sheep together. The dog makes / sure that none of the sheep get lost.

When the owner gives a command, the dog

runs at the sheep to make them move in the / right direction.

Words read correctly = _____ = _____ % (Score)

Words in sample   155
(pp. 3–7)

Copyright © Houghton Mifflin Company. All rights reserved.

Oral Reading Check

Addie's Bad Day (pp. 4–10)

Addie peeked around the tree. / She did not see anyone.

"I will be right back, Mom," / she called, / and she ran next door

to Max's house. / Addie pulled her hat down.

Then she peeked in the window. / "RUFF, RUFF," barked Ginger, / Max's dog.

The door opened. / "It's me," said Addie. / "Happy birthday, Max."

"I knew it was you," said Max. / "Come in, Addie."

"I will only stay a minute," / said Addie. / "Here is your birthday card,

and here is your present." / "Thank you," said Max.

"You are early for the party, / but you can stay."

"No, I can't stay," said Addie. / "Why not?" asked Max.

"It is a bad day," said Addie. / "Read your birthday card,

and you will see why." / Max opened the card and read:

HAPPY BIRTHDAY, MAX. / THE LEAVES FALL HERE.

THE LEAVES FALL THERE. / THE TREE IS BARE. / POOR TREE. / POOR ME.

I CANNOT COME TO YOUR / BIRTHDAY PARTY. / LOVE, ADDIE.

Copyright © Houghton Mifflin Company. All rights reserved.

Words read correctly = _____ = _____ % (Score)

Words in sample   155

(pp. 4–10)

Oral Reading Check

Name _____ **Date** _____

The Grandma Mix-up (pp. 7-17)

The Mix-up / Pip's mom and dad were taking a trip.

"We will be gone / two days and two nights," / said Pip's mom.

"Grandma Nan / will take care of you."

Mom and Dad and Pip / went downstairs / to wait for Grandma Nan.

"Here she comes!" cried Pip. / "Hi, Grandma Nan!"

"Hello, hello," said Grandma Nan. / "How is my good grandchild?"

Just then / a taxi raced up.

Out popped Grandma Sal. / "Here I am," she called.

"Did you ask Grandma Sal to baby-sit?" / Mom asked Dad.

"Did you ask Grandma Nan to baby-sit?" / Dad asked Mom.

"Now what will we do?" / "No matter," said Grandma Sal.

"We can both baby-sit!" / "Are you sure?" asked Dad.

"Run along," said Grandma Sal. / "We will have a fine time."

"Good-bye, Pip," said Dad. / "We will miss you," said Mom.

They hugged Pip good-bye / and rode away in a taxi.

Words read correctly = _____ = _____ % (Score)
Words in sample   150
(pp. 7-17)

Copyright © Houghton Mifflin Company. All rights reserved.

Oral Reading Check

Name _____ **Date** _____

Frog and Toad All Year (pp. 4–9)

Down the Hill / Frog knocked at Toad's door. / "Toad, wake up," he cried.

"Come out and see / how wonderful the winter is!"

"I will not," said Toad. / "I am in my warm bed." / "Winter is beautiful,"

said Frog. / "Come out and have fun." / "Blah," said Toad.

"I do not have / any winter clothes." / Frog came into the house.

"I have brought you / some things to wear," he said. / Frog pushed a coat

down over the top of Toad. / Frog pulled snowpants

up over the bottom of Toad. / He put a hat and scarf / on Toad's head.

"Help!" cried Toad. / "My best friend / is trying to kill me!"

"I am only getting you ready / for winter," said Frog.

Frog and Toad went outside. / They tramped through the snow.

"We will ride / down this big hill / on my sled," said Frog.

"Not me," said Toad. / "Do not be afraid," said Frog. / "I will be with you

on the sled. / It will be a fine, fast ride. / Toad, you sit in front.

I will sit right behind you." / The sled began to move / down the hill.

"Here we go!" / said Frog.

Words read correctly = _____ = _____ % (Score)

Words in sample   **188**
(pp. 4–9)

Copyright © Houghton Mifflin Company. All rights reserved.

Oral Reading Check

Name _____ Date _____

Frog and Toad Together (pp. 4–10)

A List / One morning Toad sat in bed. / "I have many things to do," he said.

"I will write them / all down on a list / so that I can remember them."

Toad wrote on a piece of paper: / A list of things to do today

Then he wrote: / Wake up / "I have done that," said Toad,

and he crossed out: / Wake up / Then Toad wrote other things on the paper.

"There," said Toad. / "Now my day is all written down." / He got out of bed

and had something to eat. / Then Toad crossed out: / Eat Breakfast

Toad took his clothes / out of the closet / and put them on.

Then he crossed out: / Get Dressed / Toad put the list in his pocket.

He opened the door / and walked out into the morning.

Soon Toad was at Frog's front door. / He took the list from his pocket

and crossed out: / Go to Frog's House / Toad knocked at the door.

"Hello," said Frog. / "Look at my list / of things to do," / said Toad.

"Oh," said Frog, / "that is very nice." / Toad said, "My list tells me

that we will go / for a walk." / "All right," said Frog. / "I am ready."

Copyright © Houghton Mifflin Company. All rights reserved.

Words read correctly = _____ = _____ % (Score)

Words in sample   **197**
(pp. 4–10)

Oral Reading Check

Name _____ Date _____

Too Many Babas *(pp. 7–16)*

Baba Edis lived / in a little wooden house / at the edge of town.

One morning when she woke up, / it was very cold.

"This is a good day / to make some soup to warm my bones,"

Baba Edis said as she put on / her woolen dress and stockings.

She got out her big, old soup pot, / filled it with water,

and set it on the stove to boil. / "Now let us see what I have,"

said Baba Edis. / There was a bone she had saved / and a cup of beans,

some carrots, celery, cabbage, / and a yellow onion for flavor.

As the soup began to cook, / it filled the air / with a fine aroma.

Baba Basha, who was passing by, / got a whiff of the good smell

and stopped in. / "What is that delicious smell?" / called Baba Basha.

"Just some soup / to warm my bones / on this cold day," / said Baba Edis.

"You are welcome / to have a bowl / when it is ready."

"I think I will," / said Baba Basha. / Baba Basha took a taste.

"It needs salt, dear," she said, / and dumped a fistful of salt / into the pot.

Then she tasted it again. / "That's better," / she said, and sat down.

Words read correctly = _____ = _____ % (Score)

Words in sample   202

(pp. 7–16)

Copyright © Houghton Mifflin Company. All rights reserved.

Oral Reading Check

Name _____ **Date** _____

Zack's Alligator *(pp. 5–14)*

A big box came in the mail for Zack. / It was from Zack's uncle Jim

in Florida. / Zack shook the box. / What could it be? he wondered.

He untied the bow / and ripped off the paper.

There was another box inside. / Zack lifted the lid.

Inside was an alligator key chain, / with a note from Uncle Jim.

It said, / DEAR ZACK, / HERE IS A PRESENT / FOR YOU.

HAVE FUN! / LOVE, / YOUR UNCLE JIM / P.S. WATER BRIDGET.

Zack held up the key chain. / "This must be Bridget," he said.

Zack put Bridget in the sink / and turned on the faucet.

Bridget began to move— / her head turned, / her tail curled.

Bridget grew bigger / and bigger. / Soon she filled the sink.

Zack moved Bridget to the tub / and turned on the shower.

Bridget stretched and sighed. / "That feels *so* good!" she said.

Zack watched. / Bridget grew larger / and larger.

She grew out of the tub / and over the side. / Bridget moaned and groaned

and whipped her tail. / She splashed water everywhere.

Words read correctly = _____ = _____ % (Score)
Words in sample   **170**
(pp. 5–14)

Copyright © Houghton Mifflin Company. All rights reserved.

Oral Reading Check

Name _____ Date _____

Here Comes the Strikeout *(pp. 6–17)*

In the spring / the birds sing. / The grass is green. / Boys and girls

run to play / BASEBALL. / Bobby plays baseball too.

He can run the bases fast. / He can slide. / He can catch the ball.

But he cannot / hit the ball. / He has *never* / hit the ball.

"Twenty times at bat / and twenty strikeouts," / said Bobby.

"I am in a bad slump." / "Next time try my / good-luck bat," / said Willie.

"Thank you," said Bobby. / "I hope it will help me / get a hit."

"Boo, Bobby," / yelled the other team. / "Easy out. / Easy out.

Here comes the strikeout." / "He can't hit." / "Give him the fast ball."

Bobby stood at home plate / and waited. / The first pitch / was a fast ball.

"Strike one." / The next pitch / was very slow. / Bobby swung hard,

but he missed. / "Strike two." / "Boo! Strike him out!"

"I will hit it this time," / said Bobby. / He stepped out

of the batter's box. / He tapped the lucky bat / on the ground.

He stepped back / into the batter's box. / He waited for the pitch.

Words read correctly = _____ = _____ % (Score)

Words in sample   **175**

(pp. 6–17)

Copyright © Houghton Mifflin Company. All rights reserved.

Oral Reading Check

Jamaica and Brianna (pp. 5–9)

"Do I have to wear Ossie's boots?" / Jamaica asked her mother.

"Until I have a chance to buy you new / boots," her mother said.

Jamaica pulled on Ossie's old gray boots. "I don't want to wear these boots.

They're boy boots."

Her father shook his head. "They're unisex boots, for boys or girls."

"But they're too tight."

Her mother scrunched the toe of the boot. "They fit fine for now," she said.

Jamaica slopped through the wet snow to the bus stop. She

looked at a tiny hole on the toe of Ossie's right boot. Maybe the

hole would get bigger. Then she would have to get new boots.

Jamaica's friend Brianna was already there. "Hi," she shouted.

Then she said, "Jamaica, you're wearing boy boots!"

Brianna's boots were pink with fuzzy white cuffs. They weren't

brand new, but they still looked good.

Jamaica shrugged. She wished that Brianna didn't talk so loud.

Everyone would notice.

Words read correctly = _____ = _____ % (Score)

Words in sample   **156**

(pp. 5–9)

Copyright © Houghton Mifflin Company. All rights reserved.

Oral Reading Check

Name _____ **Date** _____

Thank You, Amelia Bedelia (pp. 6–15)

Mrs. Rogers was all in a dither. / "Great-Aunt Myra / is coming today."

"Now, that is nice," / said Amelia Bedelia. / "I do love company."

"We've been trying for years / to get her to visit," / said Mrs. Rogers,

"but Great-Aunt Myra says / the only place she feels at home / is at home.

So everything must be exactly right. / We do want her to be happy here."

"Now don't you worry your head," / said Amelia Bedelia.

"I'll fix everything. / What should I do first?" / "Well, the guest room

must be made ready. / Strip the sheets off the bed. / Remake it

with the new rosebud sheets," / said Mrs. Rogers.

"Thank goodness you're here." / Amelia Bedelia went

to the guest room. / "These folks do have odd ways.

Imagine stripping sheets / after you use them."

Amelia Bedelia shook her head. / But she stripped those sheets.

Amelia Bedelia had just finished / when the doorbell rang.

"That must be the laundryman / with Mr. Rogers's shirts,"

called Mrs. Rogers.

Words read correctly =	_____	= _____	% (Score)
Words in sample	162		

(pp. 6–15)

Copyright © Houghton Mifflin Company. All rights reserved.

Oral Reading Check

Name _____ Date _____

Amelia Bedelia and the Surprise Shower (pp. 4–11)

There was a knock on the back door.

"Coming, coming," / called Amelia Bedelia. / She opened the door.

"Oh, it's you, Cousin Alcolu," / she said. "Do come in."

"Mrs. Rogers asked me / to help out today," said Alcolu.

"Is she having a party or something?" / "Every Tuesday," said Amelia Bedelia,

"some ladies get together. / They just sew and talk.

But today Miss Alma / is in for a real surprise.

Those other ladies / are giving Miss Alma a shower!"

"A shower?" said Alcolu. / "A surprise shower!" / said Amelia Bedelia.

"Now why would they do that to her?" / asked Alcolu. "Miss Alma is nice."

"I don't know," said Amelia Bedelia. / "She is about to get married.

They should do something / nice for her. / She can give herself a shower."

"Your folks do have / funny ways," said Alcolu.

"Say, are you cooking something?" / "My cupcakes!" said Amelia Bedelia.

She ran to the oven. / "Just right," she said. / "They need to cool a bit.

Then I will ice them."

Words read correctly = _____ = _____ % (Score)

Words in sample   164

(pp. 4–11)

Copyright © Houghton Mifflin Company. All rights reserved.

Oral Reading Check

Name _____ **Date** _____

Bobo's Magic Wishes (pp. 4–10)

There once was a young man named / Juan Bobo. It was his job to watch the

king's sheep. / One night, the king's wheat field was

trampled. "Who did this?" cried the king.

The king ordered his men to take turns

guarding the wheat. But night after night,

the guards fell asleep and more of the / wheat was ruined.

At last, it was Juan's turn to watch the

field. Off he went, carrying his dinner and / a rope.

Juan sat in the field and ate his dinner.

Bread and honey! What a sweet, sticky / dinner! Then Juan fell asleep.

But not for long! Soon the ants came for / _their_ dinner.

They bit Juan again and again. / "Ow, ouch," cried Juan.

Finally, the ants left. But the ant bites / were so itchy that Juan could no

longer sleep. / Suddenly, Juan saw a beautiful horse

running through the king's wheat. Its

mane and tail were many different colors.

Words read correctly = _____ = _____ % (Score)

Words in sample   **155**
(pp. 4–10)

Copyright © Houghton Mifflin Company. All rights reserved.

Oral Reading Check

Name _____ **Date** _____

What's It Like to Be a Fish? *(pp. 4–12)*

Fish live in water—in lakes, ponds, / aquariums, / and even plastic bags.

Your pet goldfish can live in a bowl. You can

watch the golden fish slip over and under the

castle, hide among the water plants, and glide

quietly around in their underwater world.

A fish's body is just right for living underwater,

just as your body is right for living on land.

You can swim, but a fish can swim better! A fish's

sleek body is the perfect shape for swimming. Fins

stick out from the fish's body. They help the fish to

swim. A goldfish's tail fin pushes it through the

water. Six other fins steady, steer, or stop it.

Most fish have skin that is covered with scales.

Scales help fish to swim too. The scales are hard and

clear. They overlap like shingles on a roof. The

smooth, slick scales let fish slide easily through the / water.

Words read correctly = _____ = _____ % (Score)

Words in sample   **152**

(pp. 4–12)

Copyright © Houghton Mifflin Company. All rights reserved.

Oral Reading Check

Name _____ Date _____

A Picture Book of Helen Keller *(pp. 3–9)*

Helen Keller was born in Tuscumbia, Alabama, on June

27, 1880. She was a pretty baby. She was happy and / smart.

When Helen was just six months old, she began

talking. But a year later, in February 1882, she became

sick. She had a high fever. Her parents and doctors were

afraid she would die. / Helen's mother held her and placed wet towels on

Helen's forehead to cool the fever. After a few days the / illness was gone.

But Helen had changed. She turned away from bright

lights. She didn't hear people when they spoke to her.

The illness had left Helen Keller blind and deaf. The

world for her became forever dark and quiet.

Because Helen could not hear other people speak, she

did not learn to talk herself. She forgot the few words she

knew as a baby. Helen did things with her hands to tell

people what she wanted. Helen pretended to tie her hair

in a bun if she wanted her mother. She pretended to cut

and butter a slice of bread if she wanted bread.

Words read correctly = _____ = _____ % (Score)

Words in sample 180

(pp. 3–9)

Copyright © Houghton Mifflin Company. All rights reserved.

Observation Checklist

Date: _____

Record observations of children's knowledge and behaviors.

– = Beginning Understanding

✓ = Developing Understanding

+ = Proficient

	Name	Name	Name	Name	Name	Name
Concepts About Print						
Understands that spoken language can be written down						
Understands that print contains a message						
Matches spoken words to print						
Directionality						
Understands left-to-right in sentence						
Understands return sweep						
Understands reading from top to bottom						
Book Knowledge						
Moves from front to back of book						
Turns pages in sequence						
Finds cover, title, and title page						
Words/Letters						
Identifies a letter						
Identifies a word						
Identifies a sentence						
Identifies a capital letter						
Identifies a small letter						
Identifies names of some letters						
Identifies some words in a variety of contexts						
Punctuation						
Identifies period						
Identifies comma						
Identifies question mark						
Identifies quotation marks						
Identifies exclamation point						
Identifies apostrophe						

Copyright © Houghton Mifflin Company. All rights reserved.

Observation Checklist

Record observations of children's knowledge and behaviors.

— = Beginning Understanding

✓ = Developing Understanding

+ = Proficient

	Name	Name	Name	Name	Name	Name
Uses meaning and context (semantic cues)						
Uses context to anticipate missing words						
Uses picture cues to confirm text readings						
Uses background experience						
Uses story sense						
Rereads to confirm and self-correct						
Uses structure (syntactic cues)						
Uses sentence structure						
Uses word parts						
Uses sounds and symbols (visual cues)						
Associates sounds with letters						
Uses letter-sound knowledge						
Uses beginning and ending sounds						
Uses word patterns and families						
Shows independence and enjoyment						
Self-corrects most errors						
Crosschecks (checks one source of information against another)						
Monitors own reading for sense						
Tries to solve problems before asking for help						
Participates and discusses actively						
Finds connections between personal experience and story						

Comments _____

_____

_____

_____

Copyright © Houghton Mifflin Company. All rights reserved.

List of Books Read for Guided Reading

Name: _____

Date	Book Title and Level		Comments	Accuracy Rate*
	Early Emergent			
	1. Things I Can Do	B		
	2. The Fox on the Box	C		
	3. At the Supermarket	C		
	4. I Want a Pet	C		
	Emergent			
	5. Mrs. Sato's Hens	D		
	6. The Good Bad Cat	D		
	7. A Mosquito Buzzed	E		
	8. The Secret Friend	E		
	9. Smile, Baby!	F		
	Early			
	10. The Three Billy Goats Gruff	G		
	11. Washing the Dog	G		
	12. The Crazy Quilt	G		
	13. How to Make a Mud Pie	H		
	14. Lift the Sky Up	H		
	15. The Mystery of the Missing Red Mitten	H		
	Fluent			
	16. Nobody Listens to Andrew	I		
	17. Bookstore Cat	I		
	18. Digby	I		
	19. Mrs. Murphy's Bears	I		

*If you used a listed book to take an oral reading check for this child, record the child's accuracy rate in this column. If better than 95%, circle it.

Copyright © Houghton Mifflin Company. All rights reserved.

Date	Book Title and Level		Comments	Accuracy Rate*
	Fluent (continued)			
	20. Who Lives Here?	I		
	21. The Lost Sheep	I		
	22. Anansi's Narrow Waist	I		
	23. Bears, Bears, Bears	I		
	24. Happy Birthday, Danny and the Dinosaur!	J		
	25. Henry and Mudge: The First Book	J		
	26. Henry and Mudge Get the Cold Shivers	J		
	27. Dogs at Work	J		
	28. Addie's Bad Day	J		
	29. The Grandma Mix-up	J		
	Extending			
	30. Frog and Toad All Year	K		
	31. Frog and Toad Together	K		
	32. Too Many Babas	K		
	33. Zack's Alligator	K		
	34. Here Comes the Strikeout	K		
	35. Jamaica and Brianna	K		
	36. Thank You, Amelia Bedelia	L		
	37. Amelia Bedelia and the Surprise Shower	L		
	38. Bobo's Magic Wishes	L		
	39. What's It Like to Be a Fish?	M		
	40. A Picture Book of Helen Keller	M		

*If you used a listed book to take an oral reading check for this child, record the child's accuracy rate in this column. If better than 95%, circle it.

Copyright © Houghton Mifflin Company. All rights reserved.

Informal Observation Record

Group: _____   **Date:** _____

Name	Observations and Comments

Copyright © Houghton Mifflin Company. All rights reserved.

Professional Bibliography

Booth, D. 1994. *Classroom Voices: Language-Based Learning in the Elementary School*. Ontario, Canada: Harcourt Brace & Co.

Clay, M.M. 1991. *Becoming Literate: The Construction of Inner Control*. Portsmouth, NH: Heinemann.

———. 1991. "Introducing a New Storybook to Young Readers." *The Reading Teacher* 45:264–73.

———. 1993. *An Observation Survey of Early Literacy Achievement*. Portsmouth, NH: Heinemann.

Fountas, I.C. and G.S. Pinnell. 1996. *Guided Reading: Good First Teaching for All Children*. Portsmouth, NH: Heinemann.

Holdaway, D. 1979. *The Foundations of Literacy*. Sydney, Australia: Ashton/Scholastic.

Smith, F. 1994. *Understanding Reading*. Hillsdale, NJ: Erlbaum.

Tierney, R.J. 1990. "Redefining Reading Comprehension." *Educational Leadership* 37–42.

Word Counts for Little Readers

LITTLE READERS

The chart below lists the number of words in each of the 40 Little Readers.
Word totals are shown in boldface type.

Early Emergent

1. Things I Can Do	**36**
2. The Fox on the Box	**36**
3. At the Supermarket	**60**
4. I Want a Pet	**46**

Emergent

5. Mrs. Sato's Hens	**51**
6. The Good Bad Cat	**65**
7. A Mosquito Buzzed	**132**
8. The Secret Friend	**189**
9. Smile, Baby!	**165**

Early

10. The Three Billy Goats Gruff	**146**
11. Washing the Dog	**84**
12. The Crazy Quilt	**148**
13. How to Make a Mud Pie	**127**
14. Lift the Sky Up	**133**
15. The Mystery of the Missing Red Mitten	**246**

Fluent

16. Nobody Listens to Andrew	**370**
17. Bookstore Cat	**207**
18. Digby	**267**
19. Mrs. Murphy's Bears	**188**
20. Who Lives Here?	**230**
21. The Lost Sheep	**219**
22. Anansi's Narrow Waist	**157**
23. Bears, Bears, Bears	**464**
24. Happy Birthday, Danny and the Dinosaur!	**278**
25. Henry and Mudge: The First Book	**823**
26. Henry and Mudge Get the Cold Shivers	**675**
27. Dogs at Work	**439**
28. Addie's Bad Day	**567**
29. The Grandma Mix-up	**954**

Extending

30. Frog and Toad All Year	**1,734**
31. Frog and Toad Together	**1,919**
32. Too Many Babas	**837**
33. Zack's Alligator	**1,229**
34. Here Comes the Strikeout	**1,275**
35. Jamaica and Brianna	**733**
36. Thank You, Amelia Bedelia	**1,078**
37. Amelia Bedelia and the Surprise Shower	**1,604**
38. Bobo's Magic Wishes	**653**
39. What's It Like to Be a Fish?	**969**
40. A Picture Book of Helen Keller	**860**